The Rookie Cook

Jean Paré

companyscoming.com
visit our  website

Front Cover

1. Cinnamon Loaf, page 39
2. Strawberry Cheese Tarts, page 135
3. Cashew Beans, page 81
4. Beef Parmesan, page 87
5. Herbed Baby Potatoes, page 83
6. Batter Brown Bread, page 29
7. Alphabet Vegetable Soup, page 74

Props Courtesy Of:
Wiltshire ®

Back Cover

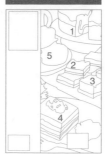

1. Sour Cream Coffee Cake, page 40
2. Nutty Squares, page 58
3. Cheesy Hazelnut Squares, page 60
4. Chilled Chocolate Dessert, page 136
5. Butterscotch Muffins, page 37

Props Courtesy Of:
Pfaltzgraff Canada

The Rookie Cook

Ninth Printing May 2004

Canadian Cataloguing in Publication Data

Paré, Jean
    The rookie cook

(Original series)
Includes index.
ISBN 1-895455-92-8

    1. Cookery. I. Title. II. Series: Paré, Jean. Original series.

TX652.P376 2002   641.5'12   C2002-900613-9

Published by
Company's Coming Publishing Limited
2311 – 96 Street
Edmonton, Alberta, Canada T6N 1G3
Tel: 780-450-6223   Fax: 780-450-1857
www.companyscoming.com

Company's Coming is a registered trademark owned by Company's Coming Publishing Limited

Printed in China

Visit us on-line

companyscoming.com

Who We Are | Browse Cookbooks | Cooking Tonight? | Home

everyday ingredients

feature recipes

feature recipes — Cooking tonight? Check out this month's *feature recipes*—absolutely FREE!

tips and tricks — Looking for some great kitchen helpers? *tips and tricks* are here to save the day!

reader circle — In search of answers to cooking or household questions? Do you have answers you'd like to share? Join the fun with *reader circle*, our on-line question and answer bulletin board. Great for swapping recipes too!

cooking links — Other interesting and informative web-sites are just a click away with *cooking links.*

cookbook search — Find cookbooks by title, description or food category using *cookbook search*.

contact us — We want to hear from you—*contact us* lets you offer suggestions for upcoming titles, or share your favourite recipes.

Company's Coming

Canada's
most popular
cookbooks!

Company's Coming Cookbook Series

Original Series

- Softcover, 160 pages
- 6" x 9" (15 cm x 23 cm) format
- Lay-flat binding
- Full colour photos
- Nutrition information

Quick & easy recipes, everyday ingredients!

Lifestyle Series

- Softcover, 160 pages
- 8" x 10" (20 cm x 25 cm) format
- Paperback & spiral binding
- Full colour photos
- Nutrition information

Most Loved Recipe Collection

- Hardcover, 128 pages
- 8 3/4" x 8 3/4" (22 cm x 22 cm) format
- Full colour throughout
- Nutrition information

Special Occasion Series

- Hardcover & softcover, 192 pages
- 8 1/2" x 11" (22 cm x 28 cm) format
- Durable sewn binding
- Full colour throughout
- Nutrition information

See page 157 for a complete listing of cookbooks or visit companyscoming.com

Table of Contents

The Company's Coming Story

Jean Paré grew up understanding that the combination of family, friends and home cooking is the essence of a good life. From her mother she learned to appreciate good cooking, while her father praised even her earliest attempts. When she left home she took with her many acquired family recipes, a love of cooking and an intriguing desire to read recipe books like novels!

"never share a recipe you wouldn't use yourself"

In 1963, when her four children had all reached school age, Jean volunteered to cater the 50th anniversary of the Vermilion School of Agriculture, now Lakeland College. Working out of her home, Jean prepared a dinner for over 1000 people which launched a flourishing catering operation that continued for over eighteen years. During that time she was provided with countless opportunities to test new ideas with immediate feedback—resulting in empty plates and contented customers! Whether preparing cocktail sandwiches for a house party or serving a hot meal for 1500 people, Jean Paré earned a reputation for good food, courteous service and reasonable prices.

"Why don't you write a cookbook?" Time and again, as requests for her recipes mounted, Jean was asked that question. Jean's response was to team up with her son, Grant Lovig, in the fall of 1980 to form Company's Coming Publishing Limited. April 14, 1981, marked the debut of "150 DELICIOUS SQUARES", the first Company's Coming cookbook in what soon would become Canada's most popular cookbook series.

Jean Paré's operation has grown steadily from the early days of working out of a spare bedroom in her home. Full-time staff includes marketing personnel located in major cities across Canada. Home Office is based in Edmonton, Alberta in a modern building constructed specially for the company.

Today the company distributes throughout Canada and the United States in addition to numerous overseas markets, all under the guidance of Jean's daughter, Gail Lovig. Best-sellers many times over in English, Company's Coming cookbooks have also been published in French and Spanish. Familiar and trusted in home kitchens around the world, Company's Coming cookbooks are offered in a variety of formats, including the original softcover series.

Jean Paré's approach to cooking has always called for quick and easy recipes using everyday ingredients. Even when traveling, she is constantly on the lookout for new ideas to share with her readers. At home, she can usually be found researching and writing recipes, or working in the company's test kitchen. Jean continues to gain new supporters by adhering to what she calls "the golden rule of cooking": never share a recipe you wouldn't use yourself. It's an approach that works— *millions of times over!*

Foreword

What makes a great cook? Knowledge and practice are two things that spring to mind. Confidence is another, and it's confidence that can turn a good cook into a great one. But even less-than-skilled "chefs" can cook with success if the right information, recipes and tools are at their fingertips.

All the crucial elements to cooking with success—experience, knowledge and practice—come together in *The Rookie Cook*. It's more than just a cookbook; it's a guide for the novice cook looking to gain confidence in the kitchen. It's also the perfect companion for the occasional cook who, for whatever reason, is suddenly thrust into the role of "chief cook and bottle washer."

Each recipe has been carefully tested and promises impressive results. The directions are clearly written and easy to follow. You'll also find a wide selection of recipes, from soups and appetizers to cookies and other treats. There's even a chapter dedicated to planned leftovers—a truly economical timesaver for busy households. Make your recipe selection with confidence because all of these recipes have been specifically chosen for their straightforward instructions.

Throughout the book you'll also find insightful tips to guide you through the cooking process. Before you begin, take a look at the *Practical Pantry*, pages 8 and 9, which identifies some basic pantry ingredients to keep on hand. The more useful kitchen utensils are pictured in the *Essential Equipment* guide, pages 10 and 11. A properly stocked kitchen can make your cooking experience a whole lot easier. Read the entire recipe and take note of what you'll need to do. If something seems unclear in the

instructions, a quick review of *Typical Terms*, pages 12 and 13, will help you familiarize yourself with what needs to be done.

Cooking should always be a fun experience, even when it's simple family meals that need a boost during the week. Sometimes cooking for others can be unnerving, but by simply telling your guests that you are new to cooking will ensure their understanding and encouragement. Relax with this collection of recipes and get cookin'—success has never been so simple, or appetizing, for *The Rookie Cook*.

Jean Paré

Each recipe has been analyzed using the most up-to-date version of the Canadian Nutrient File from Health Canada, which is based on the United States Department of Agriculture (USDA) Nutrient Data Base. If more than one ingredient is listed (such as "hard margarine or butter"), or a range is given (1 – 2 tsp., 5 – 10 mL) then the first ingredient or amount is used in the analysis. Where an ingredient reads "sprinkle," "optional," or "for garnish," it is not included as part of the nutrition information. Milk, unless stated otherwise, is 1% and cooking oil, unless stated otherwise, is canola.

Margaret Ng, B.Sc. (Hon), M.A.
Registered Dietitian

Practical Pantry

Keep a supply of these basics on hand, and you'll always be able to
make something yummy to eat from *The Rookie Cook*.

Basics

Bouillon powder
  beef, chicken, vegetable
Brown gravy mix
Buttery crackers
  (such as Ritz)
Cooking spray
Cornstarch
Dry soup mix
  *onion, onion mushroom,
  vegetable*
Fine dry bread crumbs

Flavored gelatin
  (jelly powder)
  lemon, strawberry
Flour
  all-purpose, whole wheat
Jam
  *apricot, marmalade,
  raspberry*
Liquid honey
Noodles
  *broad egg, elbow
  macaroni, medium egg*

Oil
  cooking, olive
Pasta
  *alphabet, fusilli, penne,
  rotini, tiny shell*
Rice
  brown, white
Sweetened condensed
  milk
Vinegar
  *apple cider, balsamic,
  red wine, white*

Canned Goods

BEANS
Baked beans in tomato
  sauce
Red kidney beans
Refried beans with chilies

CONDENSED SOUPS
Beef consommé
Broccoli and cheese
Chicken broth
Cream of asparagus
Cream of chicken
Cream of chicken and
  broccoli

Cream of mushroom
Mexican spicy tomato
Onion
Tomato
Tomato with basil and
  oregano

FRUIT
Applesauce
Cherry pie filling
Crushed pineapple
Mandarin orange
  segments
Whole cranberry sauce

MEAT
Flaked chicken
Flaked ham

VEGETABLES
Artichoke hearts
Chop suey vegetables
Cream-style corn
Diced tomatoes
Kernel corn
Sliced mushrooms
Sliced water chestnuts
Stewed tomatoes
Tomato sauce

Spices & Seasonings

Cayenne pepper	Dried whole oregano	Onion salt
Celery salt	Dry mustard	Paprika
Celery seed	Garlic powder	Parsley flakes
Chili powder	Ground cinnamon	Pepper
Chili sauce	Ground ginger	Salt
Chives	Ground nutmeg	Seasoned salt
Curry powder	Hot pepper sauce	Soy sauce
Dill weed	Italian seasoning	Worcestershire sauce
Dried sweet basil	Lemon pepper	
Dried thyme	Onion powder	

Baking

Active dry yeast	Cocoa	Pudding powder
Baking powder	Corn syrup	*butterscotch, chocolate*
Baking soda	Dessert topping	Quick-cooking rolled oats
Biscuit mix	Graham cracker crumbs	(not instant)
Blackstrap molasses	Nuts	Sesame seeds
Buttermilk powder	*almonds, Brazil, cashews,*	Sugar
Cake mix	*hazelnuts, peanuts,*	*brown, granulated,*
angel food, yellow	*pecans, pistachios,*	*icing (confectioner's)*
Chips	*walnuts*	Vanilla
butterscotch, chocolate	Peanut butter	Wafer crumbs
	crunchy, smooth	*chocolate, vanilla*

Nice To Have

Chocolate hazelnut spread (such as Nutella)	Instant noodles with flavor packet	Mustard seeds
		Natural wheat bran
Coarse sea salt	Jelly	Pizza sauce
Curry paste	*Concord grape,*	Ranch-style dressing mix
Dijon mustard	*strawberry*	Small fish-shaped crackers
Dried cranberries	Liqueurs	Spices
Flavorings	*almond, hazelnut, mint*	*dried mint, ground*
almond, orange	Liquid smoke	*allspice, ground turmeric,*
French-fried onions	Mango (or peach)	*tarragon*
Ice-cream topping	chutney	Stove-top stuffing mix
butterscotch	Miniature peanut butter	Taco seasoning mix
Instant mashed potatoes	cups	Wheat germ

Essential Equipment

Angel food
tube pan

Baking dish (glass)
pan (metal)

Baking sheet

Blender

Bowls (mixing)

Bread knife

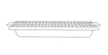

Broiler pan

Brush

Casserole

Cookie sheet

Cutting board

Dry measures

Dutch oven

Egg piercer

Electric
frying pan

Electric mixer

Frying pan

Grater

Liquid measures

Loaf pan

Measuring spoons

Meat mallet

Muffin pan

Pancake lifter

Pie plate

Pizza pan

Potato masher

Roasting pan

Rubber spatula

Saucepan

Sharp knife

Sieve

Slow cooker

Square baking pan

Vegetable peeler

Whisk

Wire rack

Wok

Typical Terms

Bake   To cook, covered or uncovered, in preheated oven on bottom or center rack.

Batter   A thin or thick pourable uncooked mixture, typically made with flour, eggs and milk, such as cakes, pancakes or muffins.

Beat   To mix ingredients using an electric mixer, whisk, fork or spoon using circular motions.

Boil   To heat liquid in a saucepan or kettle until bubbles rise in a steady pattern and break on the surface. Steam also starts to rise from the surface.

Broil   To cook on the top rack in the oven directly under the element.

Chill   To place in refrigerator until cold.

Chop   To cut food into small pieces with a sharp knife on a cutting board.

Combine   To mix two or more ingredients.

Cream   To beat ingredient, or combination of ingredients, until the mixture is light, fluffy and "creamy" using an electric mixer or spoon.

Dice   To cut food into 1/4 inch (6 mm) cubes.

Drain   To strain away unwanted liquid using a sieve.

Fold in   To gently combine light mixture into heavy mixture using rubber spatula by cutting down vertically through mixture and sliding spatula across bottom of bowl and up side, lifting bottom mixture up and over top mixture. Rotate bowl 1/4 turn and repeat until just mixed.

Fork-beat To beat with a fork until well blended.

Freeze   To place in freezer until firm or solid.

Fry   To cook in small amount of cooking spray, cooking oil or hard margarine in frying pan on medium to medium-high.

Garnish   To decorate food with edible condiments, such as parsley or fruit slices.

Grease   To lightly coat baking pan or dish with cooking spray or hard margarine to prevent sticking.

Heat   To make something warm or hot by placing the saucepan or pot on the stovetop.

12

Jelly roll-style	To roll up from one end or side, keeping edges even.
Knead	To work dough into a smooth putty-like mass by pressing down and folding in using the heels of your hands.
Let stand	To let a baked product cool slightly on a wire rack or hot pad while still in baking pan. Or, to let a mixture sit at room temperature to blend flavors.
Marinate	To cover or coat food with a marinade (seasoned liquid or paste) and set aside to develop flavor or to tenderize.
Mash	To crush cooked or very ripe foods or cooked potatoes with a fork or potato masher until smooth.
Melt	To heat a solid food (such as butter or chocolate) until liquid.
Pound	To tenderize or flatten poultry or meat using a meat mallet, rolling pin or other heavy implement.
Process	To mix or cut up food in a blender or food processor until desired doneness.
Sauté	To cook food quickly in a small amount of hot cooking oil in a frying pan or wok on medium-high heat.
Scramble-fry	To brown ground meat in a frying pan on medium to medium-high, using a spoon, fork or pancake lifter to break up the meat into small crumb-like pieces as it cooks.
Simmer	To heat liquids in a saucepan on low or medium-low on the stovetop so that small bubbles appear on the surface around the sides of the liquid and just break through.
Slice	To cut foods (such as apples, carrots or bread) into sections or pieces using a sharp knife.
Stir	To combine two or more ingredients together.
Stir-fry	To cook food quickly in a wok or frying pan on medium-high, stirring constantly.
Strain	To pour liquid through mesh or sieve to separate any lumps from liquid.
Toast	To brown slightly in a toaster, frying pan, under the broiler in the oven or simply in the oven.
Toss	To mix salad or other ingredients gently with a lifting motion until well mixed using two forks, spoons or salad tongs.
Whisk	To mix briskly with a wire whisk to incorporate air or to break up lumps.

Appetizer Bases

These golden toasted bases are a fun change from crackers. Serve them with Ham Spread, page 15, Feta Tomato Topping, page 15, or Shrimp Dip, page 24.

TOASTED CRISPS

Hard margarine (or butter), softened (optional)	3/4 cup	175 mL
White (or whole wheat) bread slices, crusts removed	12	12

Lightly spread margarine on 1 side of each bread slice. Cut bread into 2 1/2 inch (6.4 cm) circles. Press, buttered side up, into small ungreased muffin pans or place, buttered side up, on ungreased baking sheet. Bake in 425°F (220°C) oven for about 5 minutes until golden. Makes 36 toasted crisps.

1 toasted crisp: 34 Calories; 1.6 g Total Fat; 60 mg Sodium; 1 g Protein; 4 g Carbohydrate; trace Dietary Fiber

Pictured on page 17.

PUFFED ROUNDS

Package of frozen puff pastry (14 oz., 397 g), thawed according to package directions	1/2	1/2

Roll out puff pastry on lightly floured surface. Cut into 2 inch (5 cm) circles. Arrange on ungreased baking sheet. Prick all over with fork. Bake in 425°F (220°C) oven for about 20 minutes until golden. Push very high centers down until flat. Makes 35 puffed rounds.

1 puffed round: 31 Calories; 2.2 g Total Fat; 14 mg Sodium; trace Protein; 3 g Carbohydrate; 0 g Dietary Fiber

Pictured on page 17.

MELBA TOAST

Loaf of stale white (or whole wheat) unsliced bread, crusts removed, cut into 12 slices 1/4 inch (6 mm) thick	1/3	1/3

Cut each bread slice into 3 strips. Arrange on ungreased baking sheet. Bake in 300°F (150°C) oven for 15 to 20 minutes until dry and browned. Makes 36 melba toast.

1 melba toast: 20 Calories; 0.3 g Total Fat; 40 mg Sodium; 1 g Protein; 4 g Carbohydrate; trace Dietary Fiber

Pictured on page 17.

Appetizers

Ham Spread

Mild onion and tangy relish combine well with the ham pieces.
Double the recipe to use on Appetizer Bases, page 14.

Can of ham flakes, drained	6 1/2 oz.	184 g
Dijon mustard	1 tsp.	5 mL
Mayonnaise (see Coach, page 61)	2 tbsp.	30 mL
Tangy dill relish	4 tsp.	20 mL
Grated onion	1 tsp.	5 mL
Seeded and diced tomato	1/4 cup	60 mL

Mash all 6 ingredients together on plate using fork. Makes 1 cup (250 mL).

1 tbsp. (15 mL): 30 Calories; 2.2 g Total Fat; 139 mg Sodium; 2 g Protein; 1 g Carbohydrate; trace Dietary Fiber

Pictured on page 17.

Feta Tomato Topping

Serve this crunchy, toasted, walnut-flavored topping on
Appetizer Bases, page 14, or your favorite crackers.

Medium roma (plum) tomatoes (about 1 lb., 454 g), seeded and diced	5	5
Garlic clove, minced (or 1/4 tsp., 1 mL, powder)	1	1
Olive (or cooking) oil	3 tbsp.	50 mL
Balsamic vinegar	2 tbsp.	30 mL
Chopped fresh parsley (or 3/4 tsp., 4 mL, flakes)	1 tbsp.	15 mL
Salt	1/4 tsp.	1 mL
Pepper, sprinkle		
Walnuts, toasted (see Coach, page 67) and finely chopped	1/4 cup	60 mL
Crumbled feta cheese	1/2 cup	125 mL

Combine first 7 ingredients in medium bowl. Let stand at room temperature for 2 hours to blend flavors.

Just before serving, stir walnuts and feta cheese into tomato mixture. Makes 2 cups (500 mL).

1 tbsp. (15 mL): 27 Calories; 2.4 g Total Fat; 47 mg Sodium; 1 g Protein; 1 g Carbohydrate; trace Dietary Fiber

Pictured on page 17.

Appetizers

Party Meatballs

Here's an appetizer that will vanish in no time.

MEATBALLS		
Large egg	1	1
Salsa	1/4 cup	60 mL
Fine dry bread crumbs	1/2 cup	125 mL
Envelope of taco seasoning mix	1 1/4 oz.	35 g
Lean ground beef	1 lb.	454 g
RED SAUCE		
Chili sauce	1 cup	250 mL
Brown sugar, packed	1/4 cup	60 mL
Worcestershire sauce	1 tsp.	5 mL
White vinegar	2 tbsp.	30 mL
Salt	1/2 tsp.	2 mL

Meatballs: Beat egg and salsa in medium bowl using fork. Stir in bread crumbs and taco seasoning mix. Mix in ground beef. Shape into 1 inch (2.5 cm) balls. Arrange on greased baking sheet. Bake in 350°F (175°C) oven for 15 to 20 minutes until beef is no longer pink in center. Makes 40 meatballs.

Red Sauce: Combine all 5 ingredients in large saucepan. Heat and stir on medium until boiling. Makes 1 cup (250 mL) sauce. Reduce heat. Add meatballs. Simmer for about 3 minutes until meatballs are heated through. Makes 40 meatballs with sauce.

1 meatball with sauce: 242 Calories; 10.1 g Total Fat; 1018 mg Sodium; 14 g Protein; 25 g Carbohydrate; 3 g Dietary Fiber

Pictured on page 18.

Cold Appetizers

Props Courtesy Of: Cherison Enterprises Inc.

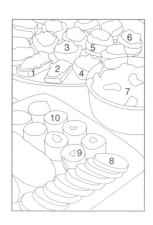

Appetizers

Cheese Roll

The paprika and chili coating give this cheese log an elegant look.
The nuts add a nice crunch to the creamy texture.

Grated sharp Cheddar cheese, room temperature	2 cups	500 mL
Block of cream cheese, softened	4 oz.	125 g
Worcestershire sauce	1/4 tsp.	1 mL
Hot pepper sauce	1/4 tsp.	1 mL
Brazil nuts (or pecans), chopped	1 cup	250 mL
Paprika	2 tsp.	10 mL
Chili powder	2 tsp.	10 mL

Mix first 4 ingredients well in medium bowl.

Work in nuts with hands. Divide in half. Form each portion into 1 1/4 × 6 inch (3 × 15 cm) log.

Combine paprika and chili powder in shallow dish or on waxed paper. Roll logs in spice mixture to coat well. Cover with plastic wrap. Chill for at least 2 hours. Cut into 1/4 inch (6 mm) slices. Makes 2 logs, each cutting into 24 slices, for a total of 48 slices.

1 slice: 50 Calories; 4.6 g Total Fat; 40 mg Sodium; 2 g Protein; 1 g Carbohydrate; trace Dietary Fiber

Pictured on page 17.

Hot Appetizers

1. Party Meatballs, page 16
2. Hot Wings, page 21
3. Curried Beef Samosas, page 20
4. Curried Beef Tarts, page 20

Props Courtesy Of: Sears Canada

Curried Beef Tarts

If you are a curry lover, add more of this distinctive spice to suit your taste.

Lean ground beef	1 lb.	454 g
Medium onion, chopped	1	1
Curry powder	2 tsp.	10 mL
All-purpose flour	1 tbsp.	15 mL
Water	1/3 cup	75 mL
Large eggs, fork-beaten	3	3
Finely crumbled feta cheese	1 cup	250 mL
White vinegar	1 tbsp.	15 mL
Salt	3/4 tsp.	4 mL
Pepper	1/4 tsp.	1 mL
Large unbaked frozen tart shells (or 54 mini)	36	36

Scramble-fry ground beef and onion in frying pan on medium-high for 5 minutes until beef is no longer pink. Drain.

Reduce heat to medium. Sprinkle beef mixture with curry powder. Heat and stir for 1 minute.

Sprinkle flour over beef mixture. Stir well. Add water. Heat and stir until boiling and thickened.

Add next 5 ingredients. Stir. Makes 3 1/2 cups (875 mL) filling.

Fill tart shells 3/4 full. Bake in 350°F (175°C) oven for 30 to 35 minutes until golden. Makes 3 dozen tarts.

1 tart: 104 Calories; 6.6 g Total Fat; 193 mg Sodium; 4 g Protein; 7 g Carbohydrate; trace Dietary Fiber

Pictured on page 18.

CURRIED BEEF SAMOSAS: Mash filling and 1 can of drained cooked lentils together in small bowl. Add 1 1/2 cups (375 mL) frozen peas, thawed, and 3 tbsp. (50 mL) chopped fresh mint (optional). Makes 4 1/2 cups (1.1 L) filling.

(continued on next page)

Roll out 1 1/2 recipes of Cooking Oil Pastry, page 141, or a mix (enough for three 2 crust pies), to 1/8 inch (3 mm) thickness on lightly floured surface. Cut into 3 1/2 inch (9 cm) squares.

Place 1 tbsp. (15 mL) filling on each pastry square. Fold diagonally. Press dampened edges with floured fork to seal tightly. Poke top of samosas once or twice. Place on ungreased baking sheet. Bake in 350°F (175°C) oven for 20 minutes until golden. Serve warm or at room temperature. Makes 6 dozen samosas.

Pictured on page 18.

Hot Wings

The sticky, spicy coating on these wings makes for tasty finger licking!

Soy sauce	1/3 cup	75 mL
Brown sugar, packed	1/3 cup	75 mL
Ketchup	1/3 cup	75 mL
Hot pepper sauce (or 1 tsp., 5 mL, cayenne pepper)	2 – 3 tbsp.	30 – 50 mL
Chicken drumettes (or whole wings, see Note)	3 lbs.	1.4 kg

Mix first 4 ingredients in small bowl.

Arrange drumettes on greased foil-lined baking sheet. Brush with soy sauce mixture. Bake in 350°F (175°C) oven for 20 minutes. Brush with remaining soy sauce mixture. Bake for about 25 minutes until tender. Makes about 24 wings.

1 wing: 87 Calories; 4.9 g Total Fat; 338 mg Sodium; 6 g Protein; 4 g Carbohydrate; trace Dietary Fiber

Pictured on page 18.

TERIYAKI WINGS: Omit hot pepper sauce. Add 2 1/2 tbsp. (37 mL) white vinegar.

Note: If using whole chicken wings, remove wing tips and discard. Cut remaining portion of wings apart at joint to make 2 sections. 3 lbs. (1.4 kg) whole chicken wings makes about 36 pieces.

Beef Rolls

This popular appetizer combines the complementary flavors of beef, onion and horseradish in a cream cheese roll.

Block of cream cheese, softened	8 oz.	250 g
Dried chives	2 tsp.	10 mL
Onion powder	1/8 tsp.	0.5 mL
Onion salt	1/8 tsp.	0.5 mL
Prepared horseradish	1 tbsp.	15 mL
Worcestershire sauce	1/8 tsp.	0.5 mL
Deli beef slices (about 8 oz., 225 g)	8	8

Mix first 6 ingredients in medium bowl until well combined.

Spread about 2 tbsp. (30 mL) cream cheese mixture over each beef slice. Tightly roll up each slice, jelly roll-style, from short side. Cover. Chill for about 2 hours until filling is firm. Cut into 3/4 inch (2 cm) pieces. Makes about 40 pieces.

1 piece: 32 Calories; 2.5 g Total Fat; 30 mg Sodium; 2 g Protein; trace Carbohydrate; trace Dietary Fiber

Pictured on page 17.

DILL BEEF ROLLS: Place small dill pickle on cream cheese mixture. Tightly roll up each slice around pickle, jelly roll-style, from short side.

Pictured on page 17.

Balsamic Bread Dip

Enjoy the wonderful flavor of balsamic vinegar in this trendy dip. Serve with Focaccia, page 33, cut into thick slices.

Olive oil (not cooking oil)	1/4 cup	60 mL
Balsamic vinegar	1/4 cup	60 mL

Pour olive oil onto plate, large saucer or shallow dish. Pour vinegar over top. Swirl slightly using tip of knife. Makes 1/2 cup (125 mL).

2 tbsp. (30 mL): 86 Calories; 9.6 g Total Fat; trace Sodium; trace Protein; 38 g Carbohydrate; trace Dietary Fiber

Pictured on page 72.

Appetizers

Cool Fruit Dip

This creamy, fluffy dip adds a touch of fun and refreshment to fruit.
Serve with strawberries, grapes, melon or any other fruit.

Marshmallow créme	3/4 cup	175 mL
Sour cream	1/2 cup	125 mL
Brown sugar, packed	1 tbsp.	15 mL
Vanilla	1/2 tsp.	2 mL
Frozen whipped topping, thawed	2 cups	500 mL

Beat marshmallow créme, sour cream, brown sugar and vanilla together in medium bowl until blended and brown sugar is dissolved.

Fold in whipped topping. Makes 2 1/2 cups (625 mL).

2 tbsp. (30 mL): 47 Calories; 2.8 g Total Fat; 6 mg Sodium; trace Protein; 5 g Carbohydrate; 0 g Dietary Fiber

Pictured on page 54.

Artichoke Dip

This mildly spicy dip is chockful of artichokes.
A sprinkling of paprika makes it attractive as well as tasty.

Can of artichoke hearts, drained, chopped and mashed with fork	14 oz.	398 mL
Mayonnaise (see Coach, page 61)	1/2 cup	125 mL
Worcestershire sauce	1 tsp.	5 mL
Cayenne pepper	1/16 tsp.	0.5 mL
Onion powder	1/2 tsp.	2 mL
Drops of liquid smoke (optional)	1 – 2	1 – 2
Paprika, sprinkle		

Mix first 6 ingredients well in shallow dish. Chill.

Just before serving, sprinkle with paprika. Makes 1 1/2 cups (375 mL).

2 tbsp. (30 mL): 77 Calories; 7.5 g Total Fat; 110 mg Sodium; 1 g Protein; 2 g Carbohydrate; 1 g Dietary Fiber

Shrimp Dip

This dip is very good served with Appetizer Bases, page 14.
Use what is left over as a dip for crackers or chips.

Block of cream cheese, softened	8 oz.	250 g
Salad dressing (or mayonnaise), see Coach, page 61	2/3 cup	150 mL
Chili sauce	2 tbsp.	30 mL
Sweet pickle relish	1 tbsp.	15 mL
Lemon juice	1 tsp.	5 mL
Prepared horseradish	1 tsp.	5 mL
Worcestershire sauce	1 tsp.	5 mL
Frozen cooked shrimp, thawed, chopped	6 oz.	170 g

Beat first 7 ingredients together in medium bowl.

Add shrimp. Stir. Chill. Makes 2 1/2 cups (625 mL).

*2 tbsp. (30 mL): 92 Calories; 8.2 g Total Fat; 135 mg Sodium; 3 g Protein; 2 g Carbohydrate;
trace Dietary Fiber*

Pictured on page 17.

Little Dilled Snacks

These crispy, flavorful little crackers are a cinch to make.
They will be a hit with kids and grown-ups alike!

Hard margarine (or butter)	1/2 cup	125 mL

Envelope of ranch-style dressing mix
    (1 oz., 28 g, size), stir before
    measuring
	1/2	1/2

Dill weed	1 1/2 tsp.	7 mL
Paprika	1/4 tsp.	1 mL
Plain-flavored fish-shaped crackers	4 cups	1 L

Melt margarine in medium saucepan on medium. Add dressing mix, dill
weed and paprika. Mix well using whisk.

(continued on next page)

Put crackers into large bowl. Pour dill mixture over top. Toss until well coated. Spread on large ungreased baking sheet. Bake in 300°F (150°C) oven for 15 minutes, stirring after 10 minutes, until golden and crisp. Cool completely. Store in airtight container. Makes 4 cups (1 L).

1/4 cup (60 mL): 120 Calories; 9.3 g Total Fat; 241 mg Sodium; 1 g Protein; 8 g Carbohydrate; trace Dietary Fiber

Pictured on page 53.

Classic Caesar

A spicy clam and tomato-flavored classic!
Add a little extra lime juice for an added zip.

SALTED RIM		
Lime (or lemon) wedge	1	1
Celery salt		
Vodka	1 1/2 oz.	45 mL
Lime (or lemon) juice	1 – 1 1/2 tsp.	5 – 7 mL
Worcestershire sauce	1/2 tsp.	2 mL
Hot pepper sauce	1/8 tsp.	0.5 mL
Clam tomato beverage	3/4 cup	175 mL
Ice cubes	2 – 3	2 – 3
Celery stick, with leaves, long enough to protrude from top of glass (optional)	1	1
Small lime wedge (optional)	1	1

Salted Rim: Rub lime completely around rim of glass. Place enough celery salt in shallow dish or on waxed paper to be 1/8 inch (3 mm) deep. Dip rim of glass into celery salt to coat completely.

Combine next 5 ingredients in 1 cup (250 mL) liquid measure.

Carefully add ice cubes to salted glass. Carefully pour vodka mixture over ice cubes without touching rim.

Add celery stick and lime wedge. Serves 1.

1 serving: 190 Calories; 0.2 g Total Fat; 816 mg Sodium; 1 g Protein; 22 g Carbohydrate; trace Dietary Fiber

Pictured on page 125.

Cranberry Punch

Try this refreshing and fruity punch.
The deep red cranberry juice gives it a festive look.

Cranberry cocktail	9 cups	2.25 L
Grapefruit juice	2 cups	500 mL
Pineapple juice	2 cups	500 mL
Granulated sugar	1/2 cup	125 mL
Ginger ale	12 cups	3 L

Combine first 4 ingredients in large punch bowl. Stir until sugar is dissolved. Chill.

Just before serving, add ginger ale. Stir gently. Makes 25 cups (6.25 L).

1 cup (250 mL): 134 Calories; 0.1 g Total Fat; 13 mg Sodium; trace Protein; 34 g Carbohydrate; trace Dietary Fiber

Sangria

This traditional Spanish refreshment is a tasty blend of citrus and wine.
Perfect for a hot afternoon in the shade.

Prepared orange juice	1 cup	250 mL
Lemon (or lime) juice	1/3 cup	75 mL
Granulated sugar	1/2 cup	125 mL
Red wine	3 cups	750 mL
Club soda	1 1/2 cups	375 mL
Orange slices	3 – 5	3 – 5
Lemon (or lime) slices	3 – 5	3 – 5

Measure orange juice and lemon juice into 2 quart (2 L) pitcher. Add sugar and wine. Stir until sugar is dissolved. Chill.

Just before serving, add club soda and orange and lemon slices. Stir gently. Serve over ice. Makes 6 cups (1.5 L).

1 cup (250 mL): 181 Calories; trace Total Fat; 21 mg Sodium; 1 g Protein; 26 g Carbohydrate; trace Dietary Fiber

VIRGIN SANGRIA: Omit red wine. Use same amount of white or red grape juice or alcohol-free red wine.

Peach Yogurt Drink

A quick way to jump-start the day.
A great breakfast drink that tastes like orange sherbet!

Prepared orange juice	1 cup	250 mL
Milk	1/2 cup	125 mL
Non-fat peach yogurt	1/2 cup	125 mL
Vanilla	1/2 tsp.	2 mL

Put all 4 ingredients into blender. Process until smooth. Makes 2 cups (500 mL).

1 cup (250 mL): 129 Calories; 0.9 g Total Fat; 79 mg Sodium; 6 g Protein; 24 g Carbohydrate; trace Dietary Fiber

Pictured on page 53.

Hot Toddy

This creamy lightly spiced drink will warm you down to your toes.
Great after skating, skiing or any out-of-doors activity.

TODDY MIX

Butter (not margarine), softened	1/2 cup	125 mL
Brown sugar, packed	3/4 cups	175 mL
Icing (confectioner's) sugar	3/4 cups	175 mL
Vanilla ice cream	2 cups	500 mL
Ground cinnamon	1 1/2 tsp.	7 mL
Ground nutmeg	1 tsp.	5 mL
Ground allspice	1/8 tsp.	0.5 mL
Rum	1 1/2 – 2 oz.	45 – 60 mL
Boiling water		

Toddy Mix: Combine first 7 ingredients in large bowl. Mix well. Store in jar with tight-fitting lid in refrigerator for up to 3 weeks. Makes 2 1/2 cups (625 mL) mix, enough for about 8 servings.

To serve, spoon 3 tbsp. (50 mL) toddy mix into large mug. Add rum. Fill mug with boiling water to taste. Stir well. Serves 1.

1 serving: 320 Calories; 16.2 g Total Fat; 161 mg Sodium; 3 g Protein; 42 g Carbohydrate; trace Dietary Fiber

Mixed Ade

The color of sunshine and just as good for you.
The juice is a nice blend of tart and sweet.

Apple juice	4 cups	1 L
Granulated sugar	1/4 cup	60 mL
Freshly squeezed orange juice (about 1 small)	2 1/2 tbsp.	37 mL
Freshly squeezed lemon juice (about 1 medium)	1/4 cup	60 mL

Measure apple juice and sugar into 2 quart (2 L) pitcher. Stir until sugar is dissolved.

Add orange juice and lemon juice. Stir. Chill. Makes about 5 1/2 cups (1.4 L).

1 cup (250 mL): 133 Calories; 0.2 g Total Fat; 6 mg Sodium; trace Protein; 34 g Carbohydrate; trace Dietary Fiber

Pictured on page 54.

Mimosa

Orange juice with sparkle!

Prepared orange juice	4 cups	1 L
Granulated sugar	3 tbsp.	50 mL
Sparkling white wine (or champagne)	3 cups	750 mL

Orange slices, for garnish

Measure orange juice and sugar into 2 quart (2 L) pitcher. Stir until sugar is dissolved. Chill.

Chill wine. Just before serving, add to orange juice mixture. Stir gently.

Garnish individual servings with orange slice. Makes 7 1/2 cups (1.9 L).

1 cup (250 mL): 151 Calories; 0.1 g Total Fat; 6 mg Sodium; 1 g Protein; 21 g Carbohydrate; trace Dietary Fiber

Pictured on page 71.

VIRGIN MIMOSA: Omit white wine. Use same amount of ginger ale, alcohol-free white wine or alcohol-free champagne.

Batter Brown Bread

A slightly sweet taste with a hint of molasses.
An easy-to-make loaf that requires no kneading. Serve with
Cream Corn Chowder, page 75, or Vegetable Soup, page 73.

Granulated sugar	1 tsp.	5 mL
Warm water	1 1/4 cups	300 mL
Active dry yeast (or 1/4 oz., 8 g, envelope)	1 tbsp.	15 mL
Large egg	1	1
Cooking oil	2 tbsp.	30 mL
Natural wheat bran	1/2 cup	125 mL
Wheat germ	1/4 cup	60 mL
Blackstrap molasses	1/4 cup	60 mL
Salt	2 tsp.	10 mL
Warm milk	1 cup	250 mL
All-purpose flour	2 1/2 cups	625 mL
Whole wheat flour	2 cups	500 mL
Hard margarine (or butter), softened	2 tsp.	10 mL

Stir sugar into warm water in small bowl until sugar is dissolved. Sprinkle yeast over top. Let stand for 10 minutes. Stir to dissolve yeast.

Beat egg and cooking oil together in large bowl.

Add next 6 ingredients. Add yeast mixture. Beat well.

Add whole wheat flour. Mix well. Cover with greased waxed paper and tea towel. Let stand in oven with light on and door closed for about 1 hour until doubled in bulk. Stir batter down. Spoon into 2 greased 9 x 5 x 3 inch (22 x 12.5 x 7.5 cm) loaf pans. Cover with greased waxed paper and tea towel. Let stand in oven with light on and door closed for 35 to 45 minutes until doubled in size. Bake in 375°F (190°C) oven (see Coach, page 40) for 30 to 35 minutes until golden. Turn out onto wire racks to cool.

Brush warm tops with margarine. Makes 2 loaves, each cutting into 16 slices, for a total of 32 slices.

1 slice: 93 Calories; 1.7 g Total Fat; 159 mg Sodium; 3 g Protein; 17 g Carbohydrate; 2 g Dietary Fiber

Pictured on front cover.

Batter Pizza Bread Loaves

*These loaves are so tasty that they won't last long! Serve plain with
pizza sauce, salsa, hot pepper sauce or ranch dip or serve with
Potato Soup, page 69, or Chicken Velvet Soup, page 76.*

Granulated sugar	1 tsp.	5 mL
Warm water	1/2 cup	125 mL
Active dry yeast (or 1/4 oz., 8 g, envelope)	1 tbsp.	15 mL
Large egg	1	1
Granulated sugar	3 tbsp.	50 mL
Hard margarine (or butter), softened	3 tbsp.	50 mL
Dried whole oregano	1 tsp.	5 mL
Dried sweet basil	1 tsp.	5 mL
Grated Parmesan cheese (see Coach, page 128)	1/2 cup	125 mL
Salt	1 1/2 tsp.	7 mL
Pepper	1/2 tsp.	2 mL
All-purpose flour	3 cups	750 mL
Water	1 3/4 cups	425 mL
All-purpose flour	2 1/4 cups	550 mL
Hard margarine (or butter), softened	2 tsp.	10 mL

Stir first amount of sugar into warm water in small bowl until sugar is
dissolved. Sprinkle yeast over top. Let stand for 10 minutes. Stir to
dissolve yeast.

Beat egg, second amount of sugar and first amount of margarine in large
bowl. Add next 7 ingredients. Add yeast mixture. Beat well.

Add second amount of flour. Mix well. Cover with greased waxed paper
and tea towel. Let stand in oven with light on and door closed for about
1 hour until doubled in bulk. Stir batter down. Spoon into 2 greased
9 x 5 x 3 inch (22 x 12.5 x 7.5 cm) loaf pans. Cover with greased waxed
paper and tea towel. Let stand in oven with light on and door closed for
35 to 45 minutes until doubled in size. Bake in 375°F (190°C) oven (see
Coach, page 40) for 30 to 35 minutes until golden. Turn out onto wire
racks to cool.

Brush warm tops with second amount of margarine. Makes 2 loaves, each
cutting into 16 slices, for a total of 32 slices.

1 slice: 107 Calories; 2.2 g Total Fat; 160 mg Sodium; 3 g Protein; 18 g Carbohydrate; 1 g Dietary Fiber

(continued on next page)

BATTER PIZZA BREAD RINGS: After first rising, stir batter down. Spoon into 2 greased 12 inch (30 cm) deep dish pizza pans. Press out batter to about 1/2 inch (12 mm) from sides. Shape hole in center. Place clean, greased empty soup can in hole. Sprinkle 2 cups (500 mL) grated mozzarella cheese over dough. Salt and pepper to taste. Fold outer edge of dough into center, in sections, and press down to stick together, enclosing cheese. Cover with greased waxed paper and tea towel. Let stand in oven with light on and door closed until doubled in size. Sprinkle with 1 tbsp. (15 mL) Parmesan cheese. Bake in 375°F (190°C) oven for 25 minutes until golden. Remove to cutting board. Do not brush with second amount of margarine. Cool slightly. Makes 2 rings, each cutting into 12 slices, for a total of 24 slices.

Pictured on page 36.

Tasty Cheese Loaf

This unique version of garlic bread has a beautiful golden crust. It is deliciously rich and cheesy. Serve with Alphabet Vegetable Soup, page 74, or Herb And Veggie Fusilli, page 130.

Hard margarine (or butter), softened	1/2 cup	125 mL
Block of cream cheese, softened	4 oz.	125 g
Onion powder	1/4 tsp.	1 mL
Garlic powder	1/4 tsp.	1 mL
Cayenne pepper	1/8 tsp.	0.5 mL
Grated Asiago (or Romano) cheese	1 cup	250 mL
Chopped fresh parsley (or 2 1/2 tsp., 12 mL, flakes)	3 tbsp.	50 mL
Large French bread loaf, cut into 3/4 inch (2 cm) slices	1	1

Beat first 5 ingredients in medium bowl until well combined.

Add Asiago cheese and parsley. Stir.

Spread cheese mixture on both sides of each bread slice. Lay out long piece of foil on counter. Keeping slices in order, reshape loaf towards 1 end of foil. Wrap foil over loaf. Fold ends to seal completely. Bake in 375°F (190°C) oven for 30 minutes until cheese is melted and bread is warmed through. Makes about 15 slices.

1 slice: 197 Calories; 12.2 g Total Fat; 369 mg Sodium; 6 g Protein; 16 g Carbohydrate; 1 g Dietary Fiber

Pictured on page 36.

Sour Cream And Cheese Biscuits

These light and fluffy biscuits are really cheesy.
Serve with Cranberry Banana Salad, page 64,
Vegetable Soup, page 73, or Quick Broccoli Soup, page 76.

All-purpose flour	2 cups	500 mL
Granulated sugar (optional)	1 1/2 tbsp.	25 mL
Baking powder	1 tbsp.	15 mL
Salt	1 tsp.	5 mL
Grated sharp Cheddar cheese	1 cup	250 mL
Sour cream	1 cup	250 mL
Cooking oil	1/3 cup	75 mL

Combine first 5 ingredients in large bowl. Make a well in center.

Add sour cream and cooking oil to well. Stir until just moistened. Turn out onto lightly floured surface. Knead 6 times. Roll or pat out to 3/4 inch (2 cm) thickness. Cut into 2 inch (5 cm) circles with biscuit cutter. Arrange on greased baking sheet about 2 inches (5 cm) apart. Bake in 450°F (230°C) oven for about 15 minutes until risen and golden. Makes 16 biscuits.

1 biscuit: 156 Calories; 9.5 g Total Fat; 271 mg Sodium; 4 g Protein; 14 g Carbohydrate; 1 g Dietary Fiber

Pictured on page 90.

Paré Pointer

She had her hair in a bun and her teeth in a hamburger.

Focaccia

It is very simple to make this tender, Italian-spiced
bread using frozen bread dough. Especially good with
Balsamic Bread Dip, page 22, or Curry Soup, page 77.

Loaf of frozen white bread dough, thawed according to package directions	1	1
Olive (or cooking) oil	1 tbsp.	15 mL
Italian no-salt seasoning (such as Mrs. Dash)	1 tbsp.	15 mL
Coarse sea salt (optional)	1/4 tsp.	1 mL

Roll out bread dough on lightly floured surface to 6 x 13 inch (15 x 33 cm) rectangle. Gently transfer to lightly greased baking sheet. Cover with tea towel. Let stand in oven with light on and door closed for 35 to 45 minutes until slightly risen. Gently press finger tips into top of dough, about 3/4 of the way through, forming "dimples" all over.

Drizzle olive oil over top. Sprinkle with seasoning and sea salt. Bake in 400°F (205°C) oven for 20 minutes until golden. Cuts into 6 pieces.

1 piece: 226 Calories; 5 g Total Fat; 408 mg Sodium; 6 g Protein; 38 g Carbohydrate; 2 g Dietary Fiber

Pictured on page 72.

Paré Pointer

If you work and save all your life, someday you'll have
enough to divide among those who didn't.

Peanut Butter Loaf

*A true peanut lover's loaf. This golden loaf has a nice peanut flavor
and a crunchy, nutty texture. Make it extra special by drizzling
Chocolate Sauce, page 149, over top of the cooled loaf.*

Hard margarine (or butter), softened	2 tbsp.	30 mL
Smooth peanut butter	3/4 cup	175 mL
Granulated sugar	3/4 cup	175 mL
Large egg	1	1
Milk	1 cup	250 mL
All-purpose flour	2 cups	500 mL
Baking powder	4 tsp.	20 mL
Salt	1/2 tsp.	2 mL
Salted peanuts (or walnuts), chopped	3/4 cup	175 mL

Cream margarine, peanut butter and sugar together in medium bowl until
light and fluffy. Beat in egg. Beat in milk on low until blended.

Combine remaining 4 ingredients in separate medium bowl. Add to peanut
butter mixture. Stir until just moistened. Turn into greased 9 x 5 x 3 inch
(22 x 12.5 x 7.5 cm) loaf pan. Bake in 350°F (175°C) oven for 55 to
60 minutes until wooden pick inserted in center comes out clean. Let
stand in pan for 10 minutes before removing to wire rack to cool. Cuts
into 16 to 18 slices.

1 slice: 242 Calories; 12.2 g Total Fat; 315 mg Sodium; 8 g Protein; 28 g Carbohydrate;
2 g Dietary Fiber

Java Time

1. Sour Cream Coffee Cake,
   page 40
2. Nutty Squares, page 58
3. Cheesy Hazelnut Squares,
   page 60
4. Chilled Chocolate Dessert,
   page 136
5. Butterscotch Muffins, page 37

Props Courtesy Of: Pfaltzgraff Canada

Butterscotch Muffins

Imagine the applause you'll receive when you bring these golden treats to the office for coffee break.

Hard margarine (or butter), softened	6 tbsp.	100 mL
Brown sugar, packed	1/4 cup	60 mL
Large egg	1	1
Milk	1 1/4 cups	300 mL
All-purpose flour	2 cups	500 mL
Instant butterscotch pudding powder (4 serving size)	1	1
Baking powder	1 tbsp.	15 mL
Salt	1/2 tsp.	2 mL
Butterscotch chips	2/3 cup	150 mL

Cream margarine and brown sugar together in large bowl until light and fluffy. Beat in egg. Add milk. Mix.

Combine remaining 5 ingredients in medium bowl. Make a well in center. Add margarine mixture to well. Stir until just moistened. Fill greased muffin cups 3/4 full. Bake in 400°F (205°C) oven for about 18 minutes until wooden pick inserted in center of muffin comes out clean. Let stand in pan for 5 minutes before turning out onto wire rack to cool. Makes 12 muffins.

1 muffin: 234 Calories; 7.2 g Total Fat; 419 mg Sodium; 4 g Protein; 39 g Carbohydrate; 1 g Dietary Fiber

Pictured on page 35 and on back cover.

College Buddies Get-Together
1. Batter Pizza Bread Rings, page 31
2. Zesty Beef Casserole, page 94
3. Tasty Cheese Loaf, page 31
4. Sausage Brunch Dish, page 44

Props Courtesy Of: Pfaltzgraff Canada
Sears Canada

Nutmeg Muffins

Moist, flavorful muffins with a lovely streusel topping.
Serve with Breakfast Sandwich, page 41.

Hard margarine (or butter), softened	1/4 cup	60 mL
Brown sugar, packed	1/2 cup	125 mL
Large egg	1	1
Sour milk (see Coach, below)	1 cup	250 mL
All-purpose flour	2 cups	500 mL
Baking powder	2 tsp.	10 mL
Baking soda	1/2 tsp.	2 mL
Ground nutmeg	1 tsp.	5 mL
Salt	1/2 tsp.	2 mL
TOPPING		
Hard margarine (or butter)	2 tbsp.	30 mL
Brown sugar, packed	1/4 cup	60 mL
All-purpose flour	1/4 cup	60 mL

Cream margarine and brown sugar together in large bowl until light and fluffy. Beat in egg. Add sour milk. Mix.

Combine next 5 ingredients in small bowl. Add to margarine mixture. Stir until just moistened. Fill greased muffin cups 3/4 full.

Topping: Melt margarine in small saucepan on medium. Stir in brown sugar and flour until well mixed. Divide and sprinkle over batter. Bake in 400°F (205°C) oven for 15 minutes until wooden pick inserted in center of muffin comes out clean. Let stand in pan for 5 minutes before turning out onto wire racks to cool. Makes 12 muffins.

1 muffin: 215 Calories; 6.9 g Total Fat; 306 mg Sodium; 4 g Protein; 35 g Carbohydrate; 1 g Dietary Fiber

APPLE NUTMEG MUFFINS: Add 1 cup (250 mL) peeled and diced apple to batter. Mix well.

To make 1 cup (250 mL) sour milk, *add enough milk to 1 tbsp. (15 mL) white vinegar or lemon juice in liquid measure to total 1 cup (250 mL). Stir. Let stand for 1 minute to allow vinegar to "sour" the milk.*

Cinnamon Loaf

A treat to eat hot or cold. The ripples of cinnamon add a touch of elegance.
Invite a friend over for coffee and share a slice or two.

Ground cinnamon	1 1/2 tsp.	7 mL
Brown sugar, packed	1/4 cup	60 mL
All-purpose flour	2 cups	500 mL
Baking powder	1 tsp.	5 mL
Baking soda	1/2 tsp.	2 mL
Salt	1/2 tsp.	2 mL
Hard margarine (or butter), softened	1/4 cup	60 mL
Brown sugar, packed	1 cup	250 mL
Large eggs	2	2
Vanilla	2 tsp.	10 mL
Sour milk (see Coach, page 38)	1 cup	250 mL

Mix cinnamon and first amount of brown sugar in small cup. Set aside.

Combine flour, baking powder, baking soda and salt in small bowl.
Set aside.

Cream margarine and second amount of brown sugar together in large
bowl until light and fluffy. Beat in eggs, 1 at a time, beating well after each
addition. Mix in vanilla.

Add flour mixture in 3 additions, alternating with sour milk in 2 additions,
beginning and ending with flour mixture. Pour 1/2 of batter into greased
9 x 5 x 3 inch (22 x 12.5 x 7.5 cm) loaf pan. Smooth top. Sprinkle 1/2 of
cinnamon mixture over batter. Spoon remaining batter over top. Smooth
carefully. Sprinkle remaining cinnamon mixture over batter. Swirl with knife
to create marble effect. Bake in 350°F (175°C) oven for 55 to 60 minutes
until wooden pick inserted in center comes out clean. Let stand in pan for
10 minutes before removing to wire rack to cool. Cuts into 16 slices.

1 slice: 174 Calories; 4 g Total Fat; 196 mg Sodium; 3 g Protein; 32 g Carbohydrate; 1 g Dietary Fiber

Pictured on front cover.

Paré Pointer
There is a real shortage of truth.
That must be why it gets stretched so often.

Sour Cream Coffee Cake

A sweet surprise of cinnamon and nuts in the middle of this delicious cake.

All-purpose flour	1 1/2 tbsp.	25 mL
Yellow cake mix (2 layer size)	1	1
Sour cream	1 cup	250 mL
Cooking oil	1/2 cup	125 mL
Large eggs	4	4
TOPPING		
Brown sugar, packed	1/2 cup	125 mL
Ground cinnamon	1 tsp.	5 mL
Finely chopped pecans (or walnuts), optional	1/2 cup	125 mL

Spray 10 inch (25 cm) angel food tube pan very well with cooking spray. Sprinkle with flour. Shake and tip pan to coat bottom and sides with flour. Tap pan upside down over waxed paper to remove excess flour.

Beat next 4 ingredients together in large bowl for about 2 minutes until smooth. Pour 1/2 of batter into pan. Spread evenly.

Topping: Mix all 3 ingredients well in small bowl. Sprinkle 1/2 of topping over batter. Spoon remaining batter over top. Smooth carefully. Sprinkle remaining topping over batter. Bake in 350°F (175°C) oven for 45 to 50 minutes until wooden pick inserted in center comes out clean. Let stand in pan for 20 minutes. Run a bread knife between sides of cake and pan. Invert cake onto plate. Turn over, right side up, onto wire rack to cool. Cuts into 16 pieces.

1 piece: 277 Calories; 14.4 g Total Fat; 240 mg Sodium; 4 g Protein; 34 g Carbohydrate; trace Dietary Fiber

Pictured on page 35 and on back cover.

To get the best results when baking, *always preheat oven to required temperature before placing any food in it. Baking in an oven that is not preheated will affect timing, texture and look of the final product.*

Breakfast Sandwich

An egg, bacon and cheese favorite on a toasted English muffin.
A homemade "fast food" breakfast that's both healthy and quick.
Serve with Nutmeg Muffins, page 38.

English muffin (or hamburger bun), split (buttered, optional)	1	1
Large egg (see Coach, below)	1	1
Italian no-salt seasoning (such as Mrs. Dash), sprinkle		
Salt, sprinkle		
Pepper, sprinkle		
Canadian back bacon slice	1	1
Process Swiss cheese slice	1	1

Heat muffin halves, cut side down, in hot frying pan on medium until toasted. Transfer to plate.

Break egg into lightly greased frying pan. Break yolk with fork tines. Let egg spread out into thin layer. Sprinkle seasoning, salt and pepper over top. Cook on medium-high for 1 to 2 minutes until egg white and surface of yolk is beginning to firm.

Fry bacon in same frying pan beside egg until lightly browned. Turn egg over. Cook for 1 minute.

Layer cheese, egg and bacon on bottom half of muffin. Top with top half of muffin. Serves 1.

1 serving: 369 Calories; 17.8 g Total Fat; 1135 mg Sodium; 23 g Protein; 28 g Carbohydrate; 0 g Dietary Fiber

Pictured on page 54.

The "frying egg" trick: *A purchased bun-size ring (or a clean, empty tuna can with both ends removed) can be used to fry an egg. Be sure to grease ring well on the inside. Place in frying pan. Break egg into ring. Break egg yolk. Cook as above. When finished cooking, run knife around inside edge to loosen egg.*

Baked Vanilla French Toast

A weekend morning comfort food. Serve with warm maple or fruit syrup.

Large eggs	5	5
Vanilla yogurt	1/2 cup	125 mL
Granulated sugar	3 tbsp.	50 mL
Vanilla	1 tsp.	5 mL
Salt	1/2 tsp.	2 mL
Ground cinnamon	1/4 tsp.	1 mL
Texas toast bread slices	8	8

Icing (confectioner's) sugar, for garnish

Beat first 6 ingredients together in medium bowl until smooth.

Dip bread slices into egg mixture until soaked. Place on 11 × 17 inch (28 × 43 cm) well-greased baking sheet. Pour any remaining egg mixture over bread slices. Let stand for 5 minutes to allow egg mixture to soak into bread slices. Bake in 350°F (175°C) oven for 10 minutes per side until set and edges are golden.

To serve, sprinkle with icing sugar. Serves 4.

1 serving: 421 Calories; 10.4 g Total Fat; 936 mg Sodium; 18 g Protein; 62 g Carbohydrate; 2 g Dietary Fiber

Pictured on page 54.

Bean Burritos

Crispy bits of bacon add crunch and zip to these burritos.

Flour tortillas (10 inch, 25 cm, size)	6	6
Can of refried beans with chilies, warmed	14 oz.	398 mL
Sour cream	1/3 cup	75 mL
Medium tomatoes, chopped	2	2
Grated sharp Cheddar (or Monterey Jack) cheese	3/4 cup	175 mL
Bacon slices, cooked crisp and crumbled	8	8
Shredded lettuce	3/4 cup	175 mL
Sliced ripe olives (optional)	1/2 cup	125 mL

(continued on next page)

To make folding tortillas easier, sprinkle some water on each tortilla using fingers. Stack damp tortillas on foil. Enclose. Heat tortillas in 350°F (175°C) oven for about 20 minutes until warm or microwave tortillas individually on high (100%) for 20 seconds. Lay tortillas on work surface.

Divide and spread refried beans and sour cream on each tortilla. Sprinkle tomato, cheese, bacon, lettuce and olives over top. Fold 1 end over and fold in sides, leaving top end open. Makes 6 burritos.

1 burrito: 342 Calories; 15 g Total Fat; 651 mg Sodium; 15 g Protein; 37 g Carbohydrate; 6 g Dietary Fiber

Pictured on page 89.

Scrambled Breakfast

An uncomplicated ham and egg breakfast with mushrooms and onions.

Large eggs	8	8
Water	2 tbsp.	30 mL
Salt	1/2 tsp.	2 mL
Pepper	1/4 tsp.	1 mL
Cooking oil	1 tbsp.	15 mL
Chopped onion	1 cup	250 mL
Sliced fresh mushrooms	2 cups	500 mL
Chopped ham (or cooked bacon)	1 cup	250 mL

Beat eggs, water, salt and pepper in medium bowl until smooth.

Heat cooking oil in frying pan on medium-high. Add onion and mushrooms. Sauté for 8 to 10 minutes until onion is soft and golden.

Add ham. Heat and stir for about 2 minutes until ham is hot and slightly golden. Reduce heat to medium. Add egg mixture. Heat and stir for about 4 minutes until eggs are cooked but not dry. Makes 4 cups (1 L).

1 cup (250 mL): 330 Calories; 21 g Total Fat; 1330 mg Sodium; 26 g Protein; 9 g Carbohydrate; 1 g Dietary Fiber

Pictured on page 54.

Sausage Brunch Dish

Sausage meat gives great flavor to this easy cheesy lunch dish.
Or try one of the variations below. Serve with Spinach Salad, page 62.

Package of frozen sausage meat, thawed	13 oz.	375 g
Refrigerator crescent-style rolls (8 rolls per tube)	8 1/2 oz.	235 g
Grated part-skim mozzarella cheese	2 cups	500 mL
Large eggs	4	4
Milk	3/4 cup	175 mL
Small green or red pepper, diced	1	1
Onion salt	1/4 tsp.	1 mL
Pepper	1/8 tsp.	0.5 mL

Scramble-fry sausage meat in frying pan on medium-high for 5 to 7 minutes until no longer pink. Drain well.

Unroll and press crescent rolls together to form crust in greased 9 x 13 inch (22 x 33 cm) pan. Sprinkle sausage meat over top. Scatter cheese over sausage meat.

Beat eggs in medium bowl until frothy. Add milk, green pepper, onion salt and pepper. Mix. Pour over cheese. Bake, uncovered, in 425°F (220°C) oven for 15 to 20 minutes until knife inserted in center comes out clean. Serves 6.

1 serving: 385 Calories; 23 g Total Fat; 929 mg Sodium; 23 g Protein; 21 g Carbohydrate; trace Dietary Fiber

Pictured on page 36.

HEATED JACK SNACK: Omit mozzarella cheese. Use same amount of Monterey Jack With Jalapeño cheese.

BACON AND EGG BRUNCH DISH: Omit sausage meat. Use 1 lb. (454 g) bacon, cooked crisp and crumbled. Omit mozzarella cheese. Use same amount of grated sharp Cheddar cheese.

Bacon And Cheese Quiche

A delicious and easy-to-make quiche that will impress your lunch guests.
Serve with Spinach Salad, page 62.

Bacon slices, diced	8	8
Finely chopped onion	1/2 cup	125 mL
Grated medium Cheddar (or Swiss) cheese	1/2 cup	125 mL
Unbaked 9 inch (22 cm) pie shell	1	1
Large eggs	3	3
Milk	1/2 cup	125 mL
Skim evaporated milk (or milk), see Coach, below	1/2 cup	125 mL
Salt	1/2 tsp.	2 mL
Pepper	1/8 tsp.	0.5 mL
Grated Parmesan cheese (see Coach, page 128)	2 tbsp.	30 mL

Fry bacon and onion in frying pan on medium-high for 8 to 10 minutes, stirring occasionally, until bacon is golden. Drain. Cool.

Sprinkle Cheddar cheese in bottom of pie shell. Sprinkle bacon mixture over cheese.

Beat eggs in medium bowl until frothy. Add both milks, salt and pepper. Beat until mixed. Pour over bacon mixture.

Sprinkle with Parmesan cheese. Bake on bottom rack in 350°F (175°C) oven for 40 to 45 minutes until knife inserted in center comes out clean. Let stand for 10 minutes before serving. Cuts into 6 wedges.

1 wedge: 276 Calories; 17.8 g Total Fat; 639 mg Sodium; 13 g Protein; 16 g Carbohydrate; trace Dietary Fiber

Pictured on page 71.

Evaporated milk *is available in whole, skim, part-skim, 1% and 2%. All varieties are available in several can sizes, including 3 3/4 oz. (110 mL), 5 1/2 oz. (160 mL), 6 oz. (170 mL) and 13 1/2 oz. (385 mL). Invert can every few weeks during storage to prevent solids from settling. Once opened, store in refrigerator.*

Cheese Strata

This is a popular cheesy brunch dish that can be made ahead.

White (or whole wheat) bread slices	4	4
Grated sharp Cheddar cheese	1 cup	250 mL
Chopped cooked ham (or leftover Baked Ham, page 123)	2/3 cup	150 mL
Medium green pepper, chopped	1	1
White (or whole wheat) bread slices	4	4
Grated medium Cheddar cheese	1/2 cup	125 mL
Large eggs	3	3
Milk	1 1/2 cups	375 mL
Dry mustard	1 tsp.	5 mL
Salt	1/2 tsp.	2 mL

Fit first amount of bread slices into greased 8 × 8 inch (20 × 20 cm) glass dish. Cover with sharp cheese. Cover with 1/2 of ham and 1/2 of green pepper. Fit second amount of bread slices over top. Cover bread with remaining ham and green pepper. Top with medium cheese.

Beat eggs in medium bowl until frothy. Beat in milk, mustard and salt. Pour over grated cheese. Chill overnight. Bake, uncovered, in 350°F (175°C) oven for about 30 minutes until eggs are set and bread is golden. Serves 4.

1 serving: 385 Calories; 17.5 g Total Fat; 1245 mg Sodium; 24 g Protein; 32 g Carbohydrate; 1 g Dietary Fiber

Pictured on page 89.

Monte Cristo

Melted cheese with chicken and ham are delicious in this golden toasted classic. A great lunch with Cucumber Salad, page 64.

Hard margarine (or butter), softened	2 tbsp.	30 mL
White bread slices	2	2
Mozzarella (or Swiss) cheese slices	2	2
Cooked ham slices	2	2
Cooked chicken slices (or deli sliced chicken), to cover	3 – 4	3 – 4
Mozzarella (or Swiss) cheese slices	2	2

(continued on next page)

Hard margarine (or butter), softened	2 tbsp.	30 mL
White bread slices	2	2
Large egg	1	1
Water	2 tbsp.	30 mL

Divide and spread first amount of margarine on 1 side of first amount of bread slices.

Layer next 4 ingredients in order given over margarine.

Divide and spread second amount of margarine on 1 side of second amount of bread slices. Place on top of cheese, buttered-side down.

Beat egg and water together in shallow dish using fork. Carefully dip sandwiches into egg mixture to coat both sides. Place in non-stick frying pan. Cover. Heat on medium-low for about 3 minutes per side until cheese is melted and sandwich is golden. Makes 2 sandwiches.

1 sandwich: 499 Calories; 24.4 g Total Fat; 1027 mg Sodium; 40 g Protein; 28 g Carbohydrate; 1 g Dietary Fiber

Baby Pizzas

These pizzas are handy for lunch or a snack. The tasty combination of toppings will have your guests asking for more. Serve with Red And Green Salad, page 63.

Hamburger buns (or English muffins), split	2	2
Pizza sauce	1/4 cup	60 mL
Bacon slices, cooked crisp and crumbled	3	3
Green onion, chopped	1	1
Chopped fresh mushrooms	1/2 cup	125 mL
Grated part-skim mozzarella cheese	1/2 cup	125 mL

Arrange bun halves on ungreased baking sheet. Divide and spread pizza sauce on each bun half. Scatter bacon over pizza sauce. Sprinkle green onion, mushrooms and cheese over bacon. Broil 4 inches (10 cm) from heat for about 2 minutes until hot and cheese is melted. Serves 2.

1 serving: 303 Calories; 13.6 g Total Fat; 716 mg Sodium; 16 g Protein; 29 g Carbohydrate; 1 g Dietary Fiber

Pictured on page 90.

BABY BURGER PIZZAS: Omit bacon. Scramble-fry 1/4 cup (60 mL) lean ground beef in frying pan on medium for 2 minutes until no longer pink.

Mexi-Pizza Snacks

Pizza with a Mexican flair. Adjust spiciness to your taste by using either mild, medium or hot salsa. This dish goes well with Red And Green Salad, page 63.

English muffins (or hamburger buns), split	2	2
Salsa	1/4 cup	60 mL
Grated part-skim Monterey Jack cheese	1/2 cup	125 mL
Grated Parmesan cheese (see Coach, page 128)	2 tbsp.	30 mL
Medium tomato, seeded and diced	1	1
Salt, sprinkle		
Pepper, sprinkle		

Arrange muffin halves on ungreased baking sheet. Spread each with 1 tbsp. (15 mL) salsa. Sprinkle Monterey Jack cheese and Parmesan cheese over salsa. Scatter tomato over cheese. Sprinkle salt and pepper over top. Broil 4 inches (10 cm) from heat for 3 1/2 to 4 minutes until hot and cheese is melted. Serves 2.

1 serving: 295 Calories; 12.3 g Total Fat; 637 mg Sodium; 15 g Protein; 31 g Carbohydrate; 1 g Dietary Fiber

Pictured on page 53.

Variation: Omit Monterey Jack cheese. Use same amount of Monterey Jack With Jalapeño cheese.

Alcohol Substitutions:
- ✔ For champagne—use ginger ale or alcohol-free white wine.
- ✔ For red wine—use alcohol-free red wine, cranberry juice or red grape juice.
- ✔ For rum—use rum flavoring, starting with much less, to taste.
- ✔ For sherry—use alcohol-free sherry, apple juice or white grape juice.
- ✔ For white wine—use alcohol-free white wine, apple juice or white grape juice.

Egg Foo Yong

Moist, golden brown patties with subtle vegetable crunch.
These are good with or without the sauce.

Can of chop suey vegetables, drained	19 oz.	540 mL
Finely chopped fresh mushrooms	1 cup	250 mL
Finely chopped celery	1/2 cup	125 mL
Can of flaked chicken, drained	6 1/2 oz.	184 g
Finely chopped onion	1/2 cup	125 mL
All-purpose flour	1 1/2 tbsp.	25 mL
Salt	1/4 tsp.	1 mL
Pepper, sprinkle		
Large eggs, fork-beaten	5	5
Cooking oil	1 tsp.	5 mL
SAUCE		
Can of condensed cream of chicken soup	10 oz.	284 mL
Ketchup	1 tbsp.	15 mL
Soy sauce	1 tbsp.	15 mL
Sherry (or alcohol-free sherry), see Coach, page 48	2 tsp.	10 mL

Combine first 9 ingredients in large bowl. Shape into patties, using 1/4 cup (60 mL) for each.

Heat cooking oil in frying pan on medium-high. Cook patties for 3 to 5 minutes per side until browned. Add more cooking oil as needed. Makes 16 patties.

Sauce: Combine all 4 ingredients in small saucepan. Heat on medium, stirring often, until bubbly. Makes 1 1/3 cups (325 mL) sauce. Serve sauce with patties.

1 patty with 4 tsp. (20 mL) sauce: 69 Calories; 4.2 g Total Fat; 384 mg Sodium; 5 g Protein; 4 g Carbohydrate; trace Dietary Fiber

Tostado Meal

This is an attractive and fun meal. The cheese melts into the hot beans right on your plate. Super fast and super easy!

Can of refried beans (14 oz., 398 mL, size)	1/2	1/2
Can of diced green chilies, drained	4 oz.	113 g
Flour tortillas (10 inch, 25 cm, size)	2	2
Diced tomato	1/3 cup	75 mL
Grated Monterey Jack cheese	1/4 cup	60 mL
Grated medium (or sharp) Cheddar cheese	1/2 cup	125 mL
Sour cream (optional)	2 tbsp.	30 mL

Heat and stir refried beans and green chilies in small saucepan on medium-low for 7 to 10 minutes or cover and microwave in small microwave-safe bowl on medium (70%) for about 2 minutes until hot.

Place tortillas on individual serving plates. Divide and spread bean mixture over tortillas. Sprinkle each with tomato. Sprinkle Monterey Jack cheese down center. Sprinkle Cheddar cheese on either side of Monterey Jack cheese. Place dollop of sour cream in center. Serves 2.

1 serving: 422 Calories; 18.9 g Total Fat; 999 mg Sodium; 21 g Protein; 43 g Carbohydrate; 7 g Dietary Fiber

Variation: Omit refried beans and diced green chilies. Use 1/2 can of refried beans containing chilies.

BAKED TOSTADO MEAL: Combine refried beans and chilies in medium bowl. Spread bean mixture over tortillas. Place on ungreased baking sheet. Sprinkle with tomato and both cheeses as above. Bake on center rack in 350°F (175°C) oven for 10 minutes until cheese is melted and tortilla is crisp on edges. Top with sour cream. Cut into wedges to serve.

Paré Pointer

Tommy has a guitar for sale—it's cheap, no strings attached.

Peanut Butter Hide-Aways

These are definitely more impressive than regular cookies!
A tasty one-bite snack that will make you popular
with kids and grown-ups alike.

Hard margarine (or butter), softened	1/2 cup	125 mL
Smooth peanut butter	1/2 cup	125 mL
Granulated sugar	1/3 cup	75 mL
Brown sugar, packed	1/3 cup	75 mL
Large egg	1	1
All-purpose flour	1 1/3 cups	325 mL
Baking soda	1/2 tsp.	2 mL
Baking powder	1 tsp.	5 mL
Salt	1/4 tsp.	1 mL
Miniature peanut butter cups (or miniature chocolate candies in foil cups)	40	40

Cream margarine, peanut butter and both sugars together in large bowl until light and fluffy. Beat in egg.

Combine next 4 ingredients in small bowl. Add to margarine mixture. Mix until just moistened and stiff dough forms. Roll into small balls, using 1 level tbsp. (15 mL) for each. Place balls in ungreased mini-muffin pans. Bake in 375°F (190°C) oven for about 10 minutes until light golden and puffy. Remove from oven.

Peel and discard foil from peanut butter cups. Press peanut butter cups down into hot cookies. Loosen edges of cookies with tip of sharp knife. Chill in refrigerator for 20 minutes before removing from pan. If cookies are too cold and become hard to remove, tap bottom of pan several times on hard surface or let stand in pan to warm up to room temperature before removing. Makes about 3 1/2 dozen cookies.

1 cookie: 108 Calories; 6.6 g Total Fat; 107 mg Sodium; 2 g Protein; 11 g Carbohydrate; 1 g Dietary Fiber

Pictured on page 53.

Cranberry Oatmeal Cookies

A tasty variation on the traditional oatmeal cookie.

Hard margarine (or butter), softened	3/4 cup	175 mL
Brown sugar, packed	1 1/4 cups	300 mL
Large eggs	2	2
Vanilla	1 tsp.	5 mL
Quick-cooking rolled oats (not instant)	1 3/4 cups	425 mL
All-purpose flour	1 3/4 cups	425 mL
Baking soda	1 tsp.	5 mL
Ground cinnamon	1/2 tsp.	2 mL
Salt	1/4 tsp.	1 mL
Dried cranberries	1 cup	250 mL

Cream margarine and brown sugar together in large bowl until light and fluffy. Beat in eggs, 1 at a time, beating well after each addition. Add vanilla. Beat well.

Combine remaining 6 ingredients in medium bowl until light and fluffy. Add to margarine mixture. Mix until just moistened and stiff dough forms. Drop by tablespoonfuls, 2 inches (5 cm) apart, onto greased cookie sheets. Bake in 350°F (175°C) oven for 10 to 12 minutes until golden. Let stand on cookie sheets for 5 minutes before transferring to wire racks to cool. Makes 4 1/2 dozen cookies.

1 cookie: 80 Calories; 3.2 g Total Fat; 71 mg Sodium; 1 g Protein; 12 g Carbohydrate; 1 g Dietary Fiber

OATMEAL CANDY COOKIES: Omit dried cranberries. Use same amount of candy-coated chocolate candies (such as Smarties).

Pictured on page 53.

Snackin' Time
1. Oatmeal Candy Cookies, above
2. Little Dilled Snacks, page 24
3. Mexi-Pizza Snacks, page 48
4. Peanut Butter Hide-Aways, page 51
5. Peach Yogurt Drink, page 27

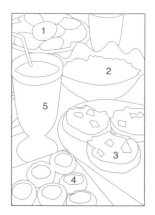

Nutty Scotch Shortbread

The brown sugar and butter give this shortbread a wonderful caramel flavor.
The nuts add a delightful touch of decadence!

Butter (not margarine), softened	1 cup	250 mL
Brown sugar, packed	1/4 cup	60 mL
Granulated sugar	1/4 cup	60 mL
All-purpose flour	1 3/4 cups	425 mL
Finely chopped almonds (or pecans or pistachios)	6 tbsp.	100 mL

Cream first 3 ingredients together in large bowl until light and fluffy.

Add flour and almonds. Mix, or work in with hands if necessary, until just moistened and stiff dough forms. Evenly press into ungreased 9 inch (22 cm) round pan. Poke holes in dough every 1/2 inch (12 mm) using fork. Bake on center rack in 325°F (160°C) oven for about 35 minutes until edges are golden. Remove from oven. Immediately cut into 24 thin wedges with sharp knife. Let stand in pan until cool. Turn out and separate. Makes 24 wedges.

1 wedge: 137 Calories; 9.3 g Total Fat; 84 mg Sodium; 1 g Protein; 12 g Carbohydrate; trace Dietary Fiber

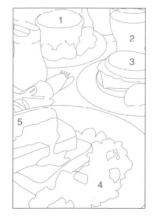

The Folks Stay Overnight

1. Cool Fruit Dip, page 23
2. Mixed Ade, page 28
3. Breakfast Sandwich, page 41
4. Scrambled Breakfast, page 43
5. Baked Vanilla French Toast, page 42

Props Courtesy Of: Linens 'N Things

Pecan Chip Cookies

Everyone loves chocolate chip cookies, especially when they have pecans too!
If you like chewy cookies, make sure you don't overbake.

Hard margarine (or butter), softened	1 cup	250 mL
Brown sugar, packed	1 1/2 cups	375 mL
Granulated sugar	1/2 cup	125 mL
Large eggs	2	2
Vanilla	1 1/2 tsp.	7 mL
All-purpose flour	2 1/2 cups	625 mL
Baking powder	1 tsp.	5 mL
Baking soda	1 tsp.	5 mL
Salt	1/2 tsp.	2 mL
Semisweet chocolate chips	2 cups	500 mL
Chopped pecans	1 cup	250 mL

Cream margarine and both sugars together in large bowl until light and fluffy. Add eggs, 1 at a time, beating well after each addition. Add vanilla. Beat well.

Combine flour, baking powder, baking soda and salt in medium bowl. Add to margarine mixture. Mix until just moistened and stiff dough forms.

Add chocolate chips and pecans. Stir until evenly distributed. Drop by tablespoonfuls, 2 inches (5 cm) apart, onto greased cookie sheets. Bake in 350°F (175°C) oven for 10 minutes until edges are golden. Do not overbake. Let stand on cookie sheets for 5 minutes before removing to wire racks to cool. Makes 7 dozen cookies.

1 cookie: 87 Calories; 4.7 g Total Fat; 64 mg Sodium; 1 g Protein; 11 g Carbohydrate; trace Dietary Fiber

Pictured on page 90.

Paré Pointer
Astronauts can't go to the moon when it's full.

Cookies & Squares

PBJ Crisps

The delicious taste of peanut butter and jam without the sticky fingers!
These crispy golden cookies are perfect with a cool glass of milk.

Hard margarine (or butter), softened	1/2 cup	125 mL
Smooth (or crunchy) peanut butter	1/2 cup	125 mL
Raspberry jam	1/2 cup	125 mL
Granulated sugar	1/2 cup	125 mL
Large egg	1	1
Vanilla	1 tsp.	5 mL
All-purpose flour	2 1/2 cups	625 mL
Baking powder	1 1/2 tsp.	7 mL
Baking soda	1/2 tsp.	2 mL
Salt	1/2 tsp.	2 mL
Finely chopped peanuts	1/2 cup	125 mL

Beat first 6 ingredients together in large bowl until well mixed.

Combine flour, baking powder, baking soda and salt in medium bowl. Add to peanut butter mixture. Stir until just moistened and stiff dough forms.

Mix in peanuts. Divide dough into 2 portions. Shape into rolls about 2 inches (5 cm) in diameter. Cover in plastic wrap. Freeze. Cut frozen dough into 1/4 inch (6 mm) slices. Arrange about 1/2 inch (12 mm) apart on greased cookie sheets. Bake in 350°F (175°C) oven for about 12 minutes until golden. Let stand on cookie sheets for 5 minutes before removing to wire racks to cool. Makes 5 dozen cookies.

1 cookie: 69 Calories; 3.4 g Total Fat; 72 mg Sodium; 2 g Protein; 8 g Carbohydrate;
trace Dietary Fiber

Enjoy freshly baked cookies anytime! *Pecan Chip Cookie dough, page 56, or PBJ Crisps dough, above, can be kept frozen, covered in plastic wrap and foil in resealable freezer bags or airtight containers, for up to 8 weeks.*

Nutty Squares

These crunchy and cheesy squares have lots of butterscotch and nutty flavor.

FIRST LAYER

Hard margarine (or butter), softened	1/3 cup	75 mL
Brown sugar, packed	1/3 cup	75 mL
All-purpose flour	1 cup	250 mL

SECOND LAYER

Mixed nuts (your choice), coarsely chopped	1 1/3 cups	325 mL
Butterscotch chips	3/4 cup	175 mL
Hard margarine (or butter)	1 1/2 tbsp.	25 mL
Corn syrup	1/3 cup	75 mL

First Layer: Mix margarine, brown sugar and flour in medium bowl until crumbly. Press into ungreased 9 × 9 inch (22 × 22 cm) pan. Bake in 350°F (175°C) oven for 10 minutes.

Second Layer: Sprinkle nuts over crust.

Combine butterscotch chips, margarine and corn syrup in small saucepan. Heat and stir on medium-low until smooth. Spoon evenly over nuts. Bake for about 15 minutes until bubbly. Cool. Cuts into 36 squares.

1 square: 102 Calories; 6.2 g Total Fat; 35 mg Sodium; 1 g Protein; 11 g Carbohydrate; trace Dietary Fiber

Pictured on page 35 and on back cover.

Peanut Butter Squares

A homemade version of peanut butter cups. A decadent layer of chocolate over a delicious peanut base. These are very rich and sweet so cut small squares.

Hard margarine (or butter)	1/2 cup	125 mL
Smooth peanut butter	3/4 cup	175 mL
Icing (confectioner's) sugar	2 cups	500 mL
Graham cracker crumbs	1/4 cup	60 mL

(continued on next page)

Semisweet chocolate chips	1 cup	250 mL
Hard margarine (or butter)	2 tbsp.	30 mL

Melt first amount of margarine in medium saucepan on medium. Stir in peanut butter until smooth. Remove from heat.

Add icing sugar and graham crumbs. Stir well. Spread and pat into foil-lined 9 x 9 inch (22 x 22 cm) pan.

Melt chocolate chips and second amount of margarine in small heavy saucepan on low, stirring often, until smooth or microwave in small microwave-safe bowl on medium (50%) for 2 minutes, stirring at halfway point. Spread over peanut butter layer. Chill for at least 1 hour until chocolate is firm. Cuts into 36 squares.

1 square: 117 Calories; 7.8 g Total Fat; 70 mg Sodium; 2 g Protein; 12 g Carbohydrate; 1 g Dietary Fiber

No-Bake Fudgy Brownies

Brownies so rich you might think they're fudge!
The nuts add a nice crunch.

Can of sweetened condensed milk	11 oz.	300 mL
Semisweet chocolate chips	2 1/2 cups	625 mL
Skim evaporated milk (see Coach, page 45)	1/4 cup	60 mL
Vanilla wafer crumbs	2 1/3 cups	575 mL
Icing (confectioner's) sugar	1 cup	250 mL
Chopped pecans (or walnuts)	1/2 cup	125 mL
Salt	1/4 tsp.	1 mL

Heat condensed milk, chocolate chips and evaporated milk in large saucepan on low for about 12 minutes, stirring often, until chocolate chips are melted. Reserve 1/2 cup (125 mL) chocolate mixture.

Add remaining 4 ingredients. Mix well. Press firmly into greased foil-lined 9 x 9 inch (22 x 22 cm) pan. Spread reserved chocolate mixture over wafer crumb mixture. Cuts into 36 squares.

1 square: 144 Calories; 6.6 g Total Fat; 51 mg Sodium; 2 g Protein; 22 g Carbohydrate; 1 g Dietary Fiber

Pictured on page 90.

Cheesy Hazelnut Squares

Dessert squares with a pleasant hazelnut taste.
The chopped hazelnuts on top give the squares a look of elegance.

CRUST

Hard margarine (or butter), softened	1/2 cup	125 mL
All-purpose flour	1 3/4 cups	425 mL
Brown sugar, packed	1/3 cup	75 mL
Flaked hazelnuts (filberts), finely chopped	1/2 cup	125 mL

FILLING

Blocks of cream cheese (8 oz., 250 g, each), softened	2	2
Granulated sugar	1/2 cup	125 mL
Large eggs	2	2
Milk	1/4 cup	60 mL
Chocolate hazelnut spread (such as Nutella)	1/2 cup	125 mL
Hazelnut-flavored liqueur (such as Frangelico), optional	2 – 3 tbsp.	30 – 50 mL

TOPPING

Flaked hazelnuts (filberts)	1/3 cup	75 mL

Crust: Mix margarine, flour and brown sugar in medium bowl until crumbly. Add hazelnuts. Stir. Press into ungreased 9 × 13 inch (22 × 33 cm) pan.

Filling: Beat cream cheese and sugar in medium bowl until smooth. Beat in eggs, 1 at a time, beating well after each addition.

Add milk, chocolate hazelnut spread and liqueur. Mix. Spread over crust.

Topping: Sprinkle hazelnuts over filling. Bake in 350°F (175°C) oven for about 40 minutes until set. Cool. Cuts into 54 squares.

1 square: 99 Calories; 7 g Total Fat; 52 mg Sodium; 2 g Protein; 7 g Carbohydrate; trace Dietary Fiber

Pictured on page 35 and on back cover.

Pearly Shell Salad

A chunky salad with shell pasta and vegetables in a mild creamy dressing.
For a tangier taste, try the variation below.

Tiny shell pasta	2 cups	500 mL
Boiling water	12 cups	3 L
Salt	2 tsp.	10 mL
Medium English cucumber, with peel, diced	1	1
Halved cherry tomatoes	1 1/2 cups	375 mL
Green onions, thinly sliced	6	6
Thinly sliced celery	1 cup	250 mL
DRESSING		
Salad dressing (or mayonnaise), see Coach, below	3/4 cup	175 mL
Milk	2 tbsp.	30 mL
White vinegar	1 tsp.	5 mL
Granulated sugar	1 tsp.	5 mL
Onion salt	1/4 tsp.	1 mL

Cook pasta in boiling water and salt in large uncovered pot or Dutch oven for 8 to 11 minutes until tender but firm. Drain. Rinse with cold water. Drain well. Return to pot.

Add cucumber, tomatoes, green onion and celery. Stir.

Dressing: Stir all 5 ingredients together in small bowl until sugar is dissolved. Add to pasta mixture. Toss until well coated. Makes about 8 cups (2 L).

1 cup (250 mL): 244 Calories; 12.4 g Total Fat; 212 mg Sodium; 5 g Protein; 28 g Carbohydrate; 2 g Dietary Fiber

Pictured on page 89.

Variation: Omit milk. Add same amount of Golden Italian salad dressing.

Salad dressing and mayonnaise are not the same product. In many recipes, but not all, they can be used interchangeably. However, salad dressing is made from vinegar and cooking oil and sometimes mayonnaise. It has a sharper taste than mayonnaise. Mayonnaise is made from egg yolks, cooking oil, lemon juice and spices and is rich and creamy.

Spinach Salad

Bright green spinach with generous amounts of bacon, egg and a complementary sweet and sour dressing. Serve with Sausage Brunch Dish, page 44, Bacon And Cheese Quiche, page 45, or Zesty Beef Casserole, page 94.

Bag of spinach, tough stems removed, cut up (about 8 cups, 2 L)	10 oz.	285 g
Bacon slices, cooked crisp and crumbled	6	6
Hard-boiled eggs (see Coach, below), diced	4	4

DRESSING

Ketchup	3 tbsp.	50 mL
Granulated sugar	2 tbsp.	30 mL
White vinegar	2 tbsp.	30 mL
Lemon juice	1 1/2 tsp.	7 mL
Cooking oil	1 1/2 tbsp.	25 mL
Worcestershire sauce	1/2 tsp.	2 mL
Onion powder	1/4 tsp.	1 mL
Cayenne pepper	1/16 tsp.	0.5 mL
Salt, just a pinch		

Toss spinach, bacon and egg together in large bowl.

Dressing: Stir all 9 ingredients together in small bowl until sugar dissolves. Makes 7 tbsp. (115 mL) dressing. Just before serving, pour over spinach mixture. Toss well. Makes 8 cups (2 L).

1 cup (250 mL): 116 Calories; 7.7 g Total Fat; 207 mg Sodium; 6 g Protein; 7 g Carbohydrate; 1 g Dietary Fiber

Pictured on page 72.

Perfect Hard-Boiled Eggs: *Poke blunt end of egg shell with egg piercer. Place eggs, in single layer, in saucepan. Cover with cold water. Bring to a boil. Reduce heat to medium. Boil for exactly 10 minutes. Drain. Quickly cool under cold running water.*

Salads

Red And Green Salad

A chunky vegetable salad with a colorful zesty dressing.
Serve with Baby Pizzas, page 47, Mexi-Pizza Snacks, page 48,
or Macaroni Tomato Casserole, page 102.

Frozen peas	2 cups	500 mL
Pickled onions, halved (or quartered)	1/2 cup	125 mL
Water, to cover		
Cherry tomatoes, sliced	8	8
Sliced fresh mushrooms	1 cup	250 mL
French dressing	1/4 cup	60 mL

Cook peas and onions in water in medium saucepan on medium for 2 to 3 minutes until peas are heated through. Drain. Transfer to medium bowl. Cool.

Add tomato and mushrooms. Stir.

Drizzle dressing over salad. Makes 3 cups (750 mL).

1/2 cup (125 mL): 100 Calories; 4.7 g Total Fat; 301 mg Sodium; 4 g Protein; 12 g Carbohydrate; 3 g Dietary Fiber

Pictured on page 71.

Blue Cheese Caesar Salad

Caesar salad with a blue cheese twist. Serve with Burger Bash, page 88,
or Biscuit-Topped Casserole, page 96.

Head of romaine lettuce, cut or torn (about 12 cups, 3 L)	1	1
Croutons (see Coach, page 86)	1 cup	250 mL
Hard-boiled eggs (see Coach, page 62), chopped	2	2
Crumbled blue cheese	1/2 cup	125 mL
Caesar salad dressing	1/2 cup	125 mL

Toss lettuce, croutons, egg and cheese together in large bowl.

Just before serving, pour dressing over salad. Toss well. Makes 12 cups (3 L).

1 cup (250 mL): 103 Calories; 8.1 g Total Fat; 221 mg Sodium; 4 g Protein; 4 g Carbohydrate; 1 g Dietary Fiber

Salads

Cucumber Salad

A cool cucumber salad with sliced onions in a creamy dressing.
Tangy and refreshing. Great with Monte Cristo, page 46.

Large English cucumbers, peeled (or scored with fork) and sliced (about 5 cups, 1.25 L)	2	2
Salt	2 tsp.	10 mL
Medium onion, halved lengthwise and thinly sliced	1	1
Apple cider (or white) vinegar	1/4 cup	60 mL
Sour cream	1/2 cup	125 mL

Put cucumber into medium bowl. Sprinkle with salt. Stir. Let stand at room temperature for 45 minutes. Put into sieve. Squeeze cucumber until most of liquid is gone.

Combine onion and cider vinegar in separate medium bowl. Discard liquid. Add cucumber to onion mixture. Add sour cream. Stir well. Makes 4 cups (1 L).

1/2 cup (125 mL): 41 Calories; 2.3 g Total Fat; 305 mg Sodium; 1 g Protein; 5 g Carbohydrate; 1 g Dietary Fiber

Pictured on page 71.

Cranberry Banana Salad

This festive red gelatin salad with banana and nuts is perfect for a holiday meal
or special lunch. Serve with Sour Cream And Cheese Biscuits, page 32, or rolls.

Package of lemon-flavored gelatin (jelly powder)	3 oz.	85 g
Boiling water	1 1/4 cups	300 mL
Can of whole cranberry sauce	14 oz.	398 mL
Medium bananas (see Coach, page 146), sliced	2	2
Finely chopped walnuts	1/3 cup	75 mL
Mayonnaise (see Coach, page 61), for garnish		
Coarsely chopped walnuts, for garnish		

(continued on next page)

Stir to dissolve gelatin in boiling water in medium bowl. Stir in cranberry sauce. Chill, stirring and scraping down sides often, until syrupy.

Fold banana and finely chopped walnuts into gelatin mixture. Pour into ungreased 4 cup (1 L) mold or deep bowl. Chill until set.

Loosen salad in mold. Invert onto dampened serving plate. (Dampness makes it easier to center mold on plate.) Garnish with dollops of mayonnaise. Sprinkle with coarsely chopped walnuts. Serves 8.

1 serving: 188 Calories; 3.3 g Total Fat; 44 mg Sodium; 3 g Protein; 40 g Carbohydrate; 1 g Dietary Fiber

Variation: Pour into ungreased 8 × 8 inch (20 × 20 cm) pan. Chill until set. Cut into squares. Serve on lettuce leaves.

Cabbage Slaw

Carrots and green peppers add a nice splash of color to this salad. It has a pleasing crunchy texture and goes very well with One-Dish Meal, page 95.

Shredded cabbage (see Note)	6 cups	1.5 L
Medium green pepper, diced	1	1
Grated carrot	1 cup	250 mL
DRESSING		
Salad dressing (or mayonnaise), see Coach, page 61	1/2 cup	125 mL
Sour cream	1/4 cup	60 mL
White vinegar	2 tbsp.	30 mL
Granulated sugar	2 tbsp.	30 mL
Dry mustard	1/2 tsp.	2 mL
Celery salt	1/2 tsp.	2 mL
Onion salt	1/2 tsp.	2 mL

Paprika, sprinkle

Toss cabbage, green pepper and carrot together in large bowl.

Dressing: Mix first 7 ingredients well in small bowl. Add to cabbage mixture. Toss thoroughly.

Sprinkle paprika over top. Makes about 6 1/2 cups (1.6 L).

1/2 cup (125 mL): 76 Calories; 5.3 g Total Fat; 157 mg Sodium; 1 g Protein; 7 g Carbohydrate; 1 g Dietary Fiber

Note: For added color, use a mixture of green and purple cabbage.

Potato Salad

A delicious mild salad with an occasional burst of sweet relish.

Medium potatoes, peeled and quartered	3	3
Water		
Salt	1/2 tsp.	2 mL
Thinly sliced celery	1/4 cup	60 mL
Finely chopped green onion	3 tbsp.	50 mL
Sweet pickle relish	3 tbsp.	50 mL
Salt	1/2 tsp.	2 mL
DRESSING		
Salad dressing (or mayonnaise), see Coach, page 61	1/2 cup	125 mL
Milk	1 tbsp.	15 mL
White vinegar	1 tsp.	5 mL
Granulated sugar	1 tsp.	5 mL
Hard-boiled eggs (see Coach, page 62), diced	2	2

Cook potato in water and first amount of salt in medium saucepan on medium for about 12 minutes until tender. Drain. Cool. Dice. Put into medium bowl.

Add celery, green onion, relish and second amount of salt. Stir.

Dressing: Mix first 4 ingredients in small bowl. Add to potato mixture. Stir gently. Add egg. Toss. Chill. Makes 3 cups (750 mL).

3/4 cup (175 mL): 312 Calories; 18.1 g Total Fat; 629 mg Sodium; 6 g Protein; 33 g Carbohydrate; 2 g Dietary Fiber

Walnut Raspberry Vinaigrette

The light fruity raspberry complements the more robust walnut flavor.

Red wine vinegar	1/3 cup	75 mL
Frozen concentrated raspberry juice	1/4 cup	60 mL
Chopped walnuts, rinsed and blotted dry	3 tbsp.	50 mL
Granulated sugar	2 tbsp.	30 mL
Pepper, sprinkle		
Cooking oil	2 tbsp.	30 mL

(continued on next page)

Put first 5 ingredients into blender. Process on high for about 5 seconds until foamy.

With motor running, pour cooking oil in thin stream through hole in lid until well blended. Store in jar with tight-fitting lid in refrigerator for up to 1 week. Shake well before drizzling over greens. Makes about 2/3 cup (150 mL).

1 tbsp. (15 mL): 48 Calories; 3.7 g Total Fat; trace Sodium; 1 g Protein; 4 g Carbohydrate; trace Dietary Fiber

Pictured on page 72.

Sesame Soy Dressing

A sweet and fragrant dressing with a bite of ginger and chilies. Perfect as a dressing for dark leafy greens or as a dipping sauce for meatballs and chicken.

White vinegar	1/3 cup	75 mL
Indonesian sweet soy sauce	1/4 cup	60 mL
Freshly grated gingerroot (or 3/4 tsp., 4 mL, ground ginger)	1 tbsp.	15 mL
Brown sugar, packed	1 tbsp.	15 mL
Sesame seeds, toasted (see Coach, below)	1 tbsp.	15 mL
Sesame (or cooking) oil	2 tsp.	10 mL
Dried crushed chilies	1/2 tsp.	2 mL
Cooking oil	1/4 cup	60 mL

Put first 7 ingredients into blender. Process on high for about 5 seconds until foamy.

With motor running, pour cooking oil in thin stream through hole in lid until well blended. Store in jar with tight-fitting lid in refrigerator for up to 1 week. Shake well before drizzling over greens. Makes 1 cup (250 mL).

1 tbsp. (15 mL): 45 Calories; 4.3 g Total Fat; 125 mg Sodium; trace Protein; 2 g Carbohydrate; trace Dietary Fiber

Pictured on page 108.

Toasted Nuts and Seeds: *Spread in single layer in ungreased shallow pan (a foil pie plate works well). Bake in 350°F (175°C) oven for 5 to 10 minutes, stirring or shaking often, until desired doneness. Use this method for almonds, pecans, walnuts, sesame seeds, sunflower seeds and others.*

Vinaigrette

A basic oil and vinegar dressing that works very well
with any assortment of fresh salad greens and vegetables.

Olive (or cooking) oil	6 tbsp.	100 mL
Apple cider (or red wine) vinegar	3 tbsp.	50 mL
Granulated sugar	1 tsp.	5 mL
Paprika	1/2 tsp.	2 mL
Onion salt	1/4 tsp.	1 mL
Pepper, sprinkle		

Combine all 6 ingredients in small jar with tight-fitting lid. Shake until sugar is dissolved. Store in refrigerator for up to 2 weeks. Shake well before drizzling over greens. Makes about 1/2 cup (125 mL).

1 tbsp. (15 mL): 90 Calories; 9.9 g Total Fat; 37 mg Sodium; trace Protein; 1 g Carbohydrate; trace Dietary Fiber

Kiwi Citrus Dressing

A summery dressing with a mild citrus and mint flavor.
A very nice dressing tossed with mixed greens.

Prepared orange juice	1/2 cup	125 mL
Cooking oil	3 tbsp.	50 mL
Fresh mint leaves, packed (or 1 1/2 tsp., 7 mL, dried)	2 tbsp.	30 mL
Corn syrup	2 tbsp.	30 mL
Lime juice	1 tbsp.	15 mL
White vinegar	1 tbsp.	15 mL
Salt, just a pinch		
Ripe medium kiwifruits, peeled and cut into chunks	3	3

Put all 8 ingredients into blender. Process on high for 20 seconds. Scrape down sides. Process until smooth. Let stand at room temperature for 15 minutes to blend flavors. Store in jar with tight-fitting lid in refrigerator for up to 1 week. Shake well before tossing with greens. Makes 1 2/3 cups (400 mL).

1 tbsp. (15 mL): 25 Calories; 1.5 g Total Fat; 2 mg Sodium; trace Protein; 3 g Carbohydrate; trace Dietary Fiber

Pictured on page 72.

Potato Soup

A thick, creamy, chowder-style soup with great potato flavor.
A real rib warmer! Excellent with Batter Pizza Bread Loaves, page 30.

Medium potatoes, peeled and cut up	5	5
Chopped onion	1 cup	250 mL
Finely chopped fresh celery leaves	2 tsp.	10 mL
Water, to cover		
Hard margarine (or butter)	1 tbsp.	15 mL
All-purpose flour	1 tbsp.	15 mL
Parsley flakes	2 - 3 tsp.	10 - 15 mL
Salt	2 tsp.	10 mL
Pepper	1/4 tsp.	1 mL
Milk	3 cups	750 mL
Grated sharp Cheddar cheese (optional)	1/2 cup	125 mL
Chopped fresh chives (or dill weed), for garnish		

Put potato, onion and celery leaves into medium saucepan. Add enough water just to cover potato. Cover. Bring to a boil on medium. Reduce heat. Simmer for about 15 minutes until vegetables are tender. Do not drain. Cool slightly. Transfer, in batches, to blender. Process until puréed. Set aside.

Melt margarine in large saucepan on medium-low. Mix in flour, parsley, salt and pepper until smooth. Add milk. Heat and stir for about 10 minutes until boiling and slightly thickened. Add potato mixture.

Sprinkle cheese and chives over individual servings. Makes 8 cups (2 L).

1 cup (250 mL): 138 Calories; 2.6 g Total Fat; 664 mg Sodium; 5 g Protein; 24 g Carbohydrate; 2 g Dietary Fiber

Paré Pointer

Cinderella can't be on the team—she runs away from the ball.

Instant Egg Drop Soup

The easiest recipe going for this tasty soup.
Egg drop soup fans will make it again and again.

Cans of condensed chicken broth (10 oz., 284 mL, each), see Coach, page 77	2	2
Water	2 1/2 cups	625 mL
Large eggs	2	2
Green onion, thinly sliced	1	1

Heat chicken broth and water in large saucepan on high for 5 to 6 minutes until boiling.

Beat eggs in medium bowl until frothy. Add eggs to boiling broth in thin stream, whisking constantly, until threads of egg form.

Sprinkle green onion over individual servings. Makes 5 cups (1.25 L).

1 cup (250 mL): 68 Calories; 3.3 g Total Fat; 780 mg Sodium; 8 g Protein; 1 g Carbohydrate; trace Dietary Fiber

EGG DROP SOUP: Omit condensed chicken broth and water. Use 5 cups (1.25 L) prepared chicken broth.

Special Guests For Brunch

1. Ham And Vegetable Frittata, page 124
2. Mimosa, page 28
3. Cucumber Salad, page 64
4. Bacon And Cheese Quiche, page 45
5. Red And Green Salad, page 63

Props Courtesy Of: Browne & Co. Ltd.
Dansk Gifts
The Bay

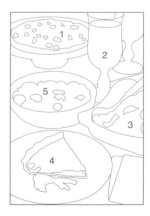

Vegetable Soup

A hearty vegetarian soup with rich tomato flavor.
A perfect winter meal with Batter Brown Bread, page 29,
or Sour Cream And Cheese Biscuits, page 32.

Water	3 cups	750 mL
Tomato juice	2 cups	500 mL
Large onion, diced	1	1
Diced carrot	1 cup	250 mL
Diced celery	1 cup	250 mL
Diced yellow turnip	1 cup	250 mL
Diced peeled potato	1 cup	250 mL
Salt	1 tsp.	5 mL
Pepper	1/4 tsp.	1 mL

Combine all 9 ingredients in large saucepan. Bring to a boil on medium.
Reduce heat. Cover. Simmer for about 20 minutes until vegetables are
tender. Makes about 7 cups (1.75 L).

1 cup (250 mL): 58 Calories; 0.2 g Total Fat; 651 mg Sodium; 2 g Protein; 13 g Carbohydrate;
2 g Dietary Fiber

Variation: Add 1 cup (250 mL) chopped green string beans or 1 to 2 cups
(250 to 500 mL) shredded cabbage.

Variation: Omit tomato juice. Use same amount of vegetable cocktail juice
or clam tomato beverage.

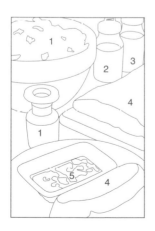

Trendy Lunch
1. Spinach Salad, page 62
2. Walnut Raspberry Vinaigrette,
   page 66
3. Kiwi Citrus Dressing, page 68
4. Focaccia, page 33
5. Balsamic Bread Dip, page 22

Props Courtesy Of: Sears Canada

Soups

Alphabet Vegetable Soup

Brush up on your alphabet while eating this colorful nutritious soup.
Serve with Tasty Cheese Loaf, page 31.

Water	8 cups	2 L
Diced peeled potato	1 1/2 cups	375 mL
Finely diced celery	1/3 cup	75 mL
Minced onion	1/4 cup	60 mL
Vegetable bouillon powder	3 tbsp.	50 mL
Medium carrot, grated	1	1
Alphabet pasta	1/2 cup	125 mL
Chopped fresh parsley (or 1 tbsp., 15 mL, flakes)	1/4 cup	60 mL
Salt	1/2 tsp.	2 mL
Pepper, sprinkle		

Bring water to a boil in large pot or Dutch oven on high. Add next 5 ingredients. Reduce heat to medium. Cover. Simmer for 15 minutes.

Add pasta. Stir. Bring to a boil. Reduce heat. Simmer, uncovered, for 12 to 15 minutes, stirring occasionally, until pasta is tender but firm.

Add parsley, salt and pepper. Stir. Makes about 8 cups (2 L).

1 cup (250 mL): 66 Calories; 0.5 g Total Fat; 829 mg Sodium; 2 g Protein; 13 g Carbohydrate; 1 g Dietary Fiber

Pictured on front cover.

Paré Pointer

The teacher asked Billy to use "fascinate" in a sentence.
Said Billy, "My coat has ten buttons, but I can only fasten eight."

Cream Corn Chowder

A delicious creamy chowder with corn, bacon and carrots. So easily done but so difficult to make last! Sure to be a favorite—especially when served with Batter Brown Bread, page 29.

Bacon slices, diced	3	3
Finely chopped onion	1/4 cup	60 mL
Finely chopped carrot	1/4 cup	60 mL
Milk	2 cups	500 mL
Chicken bouillon powder	1 tbsp.	15 mL
All-purpose flour	2 tbsp.	30 mL
Pepper, sprinkle		
Cans of cream-style corn (10 oz., 284 mL, each)	2	2
Fresh (or frozen, thawed) kernel corn (optional)	1/2 cup	125 mL
Chopped fresh chives, for garnish		

Fry bacon in large saucepan on medium-high for 4 to 5 minutes until crisp. Remove to paper towel to drain. Drain, leaving 1 tbsp. (15 mL) drippings in saucepan.

Add onion and carrot to reserved drippings. Sauté on medium for about 5 minutes until tender-crisp.

Combine milk and bouillon powder in small bowl until bouillon powder is dissolved.

Sprinkle flour over onion mixture. Stir. Add milk mixture and bacon. Add remaining 3 ingredients. Heat and stir until mixture is boiling and thickened.

Sprinkle chives over individual servings. Makes 6 cups (1.5 L).

1 cup (250 mL): 167 Calories; 5.4 g Total Fat; 713 mg Sodium; 6 g Protein; 26 g Carbohydrate; 2 g Dietary Fiber

Pictured on page 90.

Chicken Velvet Soup

A quick-as-a-wink appetizer soup. The sherry takes it from an ordinary canned soup to an elegant starter. You'll impress your guests with this one! Serve with Batter Pizza Bread Loaves, page 30.

Cans of condensed cream of chicken soup (10 oz., 284 mL, each)	2	2
Milk	1 1/2 cups	375 mL
Can of condensed chicken broth (see Coach, page 77)	10 oz.	284 mL
Sherry (or alcohol-free sherry), see Coach, page 48	2 tbsp.	30 mL
Croutons (see Coach, page 86) or fresh chives or parsley, for garnish		

Combine first 4 ingredients in large saucepan. Heat on medium-low for about 15 minutes until simmering.

Sprinkle croutons over individual servings. Makes about 4 cups (1 L).

1 cup (250 mL): 210 Calories; 10.6 g Total Fat; 1705 mg Sodium; 11 g Protein; 16 g Carbohydrate; trace Dietary Fiber

Quick Broccoli Soup

A cheese and broccoli soup that is thick and satisfying to eat and manageable to prepare. Serve with Sour Cream And Cheese Biscuits, page 32.

Can of condensed cream of mushroom soup	10 oz.	284 mL
Milk (1 soup can)	10 oz.	284 mL
Grated sharp Cheddar cheese	1 cup	250 mL
Frozen chopped broccoli, thawed, chopped into tiny bits	1 cup	250 mL
Worcestershire sauce	1/4 tsp.	1 mL

(continued on next page)

Stir soup and milk vigorously in large saucepan. Heat on medium for about 8 minutes, stirring often, until heated through.

Add cheese, broccoli and Worcestershire sauce. Heat for about 5 minutes, stirring often, until simmering. Reduce heat to medium-low. Simmer, uncovered, for about 5 minutes until broccoli is tender. Makes 4 1/2 cups (1.1 L).

1 cup (250 mL): 209 Calories; 14.6 g Total Fat; 749 mg Sodium; 10 g Protein; 10 g Carbohydrate; 1 g Dietary Fiber

---

Curry Soup

A convenient appetizer soup with a creamy mild curry flavor. This soup can be served either hot or cold. Serve with Focaccia, page 33.

Can of condensed beef consommé (see Coach, below)	10 oz.	284 mL
Block of cream cheese, cut up	8 oz.	250 g
Curry powder	1 tsp.	5 mL
Onion powder	1/8 tsp.	0.5 mL
Sherry (or alcohol-free sherry), see Coach, page 48	2 tsp.	10 mL

Chopped chives, for garnish

Process first 5 ingredients in blender until smooth. Transfer to medium saucepan. Heat on medium for 4 to 5 minutes, stirring frequently, until simmering. To serve chilled, chill for at least 1 1/2 hours. Just before serving, stir until softened.

Sprinkle chives over individual servings. Makes 2 cups (500 mL).

1 cup (250 mL): 479 Calories; 43.7 g Total Fat; 1138 mg Sodium; 16 g Protein; 6 g Carbohydrate; trace Dietary Fiber

Variation: Omit beef consommé. Use same amount of chicken broth.

Broth and consommé are not the same product but are interchangeable within recipes. Broth is a liquid that comes from cooking fish, meat or vegetables in water and is sometimes called bouillon. Consommé is broth that has been clarified (the impurities removed). Both are available commercially in cans.

Broccoli Cheese Casserole

Melted cheese and lots of broccoli make this rich-tasting side dish a sure hit!

Chopped fresh (or frozen) broccoli (about 2 lbs., 900 g)	8 cups	2 L
Water	2 cups	500 mL
Salt	1/2 tsp.	2 mL
Large eggs, fork-beaten	2	2
Can of condensed cream of mushroom soup	10 oz.	284 mL
Grated medium Cheddar cheese	1 cup	250 mL
Mayonnaise (see Coach, page 61)	1/2 cup	125 mL
Sour cream	1/2 cup	125 mL
Onion powder	1/4 tsp.	1 mL
Salt	1/4 tsp.	1 mL
Pepper	1/8 tsp.	0.5 mL

Cook broccoli in water and salt in large saucepan on medium for about 10 minutes until tender-crisp. Drain. Turn into greased 2 quart (2 L) casserole.

Combine remaining 8 ingredients in medium bowl. Pour over broccoli. Stir gently. Bake, uncovered, in 350°F (175°C) oven for 30 to 40 minutes until heated through. Serves 6.

1 serving: 364 Calories; 30.9 g Total Fat; 793 mg Sodium; 12 g Protein; 12 g Carbohydrate; 3 g Dietary Fiber

Baked Tomatoes

Zesty baked tomatoes with cheesy crumbled topping.
These are great with Beef Parmesan, page 87, and Micro-Chicken, page 129.

Large tomatoes	4	4
Salt	1/2 tsp.	2 mL
Pepper, sprinkle		
Hard margarine (or butter)	1 tbsp.	15 mL
Fine dry bread crumbs	1/4 cup	60 mL
Finely grated Parmesan (or Romano) cheese (see Coach, page 128)	1/4 cup	60 mL
Dried sweet basil (or 4 tsp., 20 mL, chopped fresh sweet basil)	1 tsp.	5 mL

(continued on next page)

Cut tomatoes in half horizontally. Trim edges in fancy design if desired. Arrange in single layer in ungreased baking pan. Sprinkle with salt and pepper.

Melt margarine in small saucepan on medium-low. Stir in bread crumbs, Parmesan cheese and basil until well mixed. Sprinkle over tomatoes. Bake, uncovered, in 350°F (175°C) oven for about 25 minutes until tender but firm. Makes 8 tomato halves.

1 tomato half: 58 Calories; 2.9 g Total Fat; 265 mg Sodium; 3 g Protein; 6 g Carbohydrate; 1 g Dietary Fiber

Asian-Style Vegetables

Fresh ginger and toasted sesame seeds give this flavorful side dish an exotic flair! The perfect accompaniment to Chicken Teriyaki, page 100, or Pork Stir-Fry, page 110.

Chopped fresh broccoli	2 cups	500 mL
Chopped fresh cauliflower	2 cups	500 mL
Small red pepper, chopped	1	1
Boiling water	1 cup	250 mL
Hard margarine (or butter)	1 tbsp.	15 mL
Soy sauce	2 tbsp.	30 mL
Brown sugar, packed	2 tsp.	10 mL
Freshly grated gingerroot (or 1/4 – 1/2 tsp., 1 – 2 mL, ground ginger)	1 – 2 tsp.	5 – 10 mL
Green onions, sliced	2	2
Sesame seeds, toasted (see Coach, page 67)	1 1/2 tsp.	7 mL

Combine broccoli, cauliflower, red pepper and boiling water in large saucepan. Cover. Cook on medium for about 8 minutes until vegetables are tender-crisp. Drain. Turn into serving dish. Cover to keep warm.

Melt margarine in same saucepan. Add soy sauce, brown sugar and ginger. Let bubble on medium for 1 minute. Pour over vegetables. Toss gently.

Sprinkle green onion and sesame seeds over top. Serves 4.

1 serving: 84 Calories; 3.8 g Total Fat; 587 mg Sodium; 4 g Protein; 11 g Carbohydrate; 3 g Dietary Fiber

Pictured on page 107.

Glazed Carrots

A sweet orange glaze with a hint of ginger makes these carrots delicious.
They are the perfect complement to Chicken à la King, page 97.

Medium carrots, sliced crinkle cut 1/2 inch (12 mm) thick	2 lbs.	900 g
Water		
Salt	1/2 tsp.	2 mL
Granulated sugar	1/2 tsp.	2 mL
Hard margarine (or butter)	1 tbsp.	15 mL
All-purpose flour	1 tbsp.	15 mL
Brown sugar, packed	2 1/2 tbsp.	37 mL
Chopped candied ginger	2 tbsp.	30 mL
Prepared orange juice	2/3 cup	150 mL
Salt, sprinkle		

Cook carrot in water, salt and granulated sugar in large saucepan on medium-high for 10 to 12 minutes until tender-crisp. Drain. Return to saucepan. Cover to keep warm.

Melt margarine in small saucepan on medium. Mix in flour, brown sugar and ginger. Stir in orange juice. Heat and stir for 3 minutes until boiling and thickened. Add salt. Pour over carrots. Stir gently. Serves 8.

1 serving: 98 Calories; 1.7 g Total Fat; 59 mg Sodium; 1 g Protein; 20 g Carbohydrate; 3 g Dietary Fiber

Pictured on page 125.

Sweet Baked Squash

The hollow of the squash holds a buttery, sweet sauce.
Serve with Simple Oven Dinner, page 106.

Medium acorn squash	2	2
Hard margarine (or butter), softened	2 tbsp.	30 mL
Brown sugar, packed	2 tbsp.	30 mL
Salt	1/4 tsp.	1 mL
Pepper, sprinkle		

(continued on next page)

Cut each squash in half lengthwise. Remove seeds. Arrange, cut side down, on greased baking sheet. Bake in 375°F (190°C) oven for 30 to 40 minutes until tender but firm.

Heat margarine, brown sugar, salt and pepper in small saucepan on medium for about 3 minutes until margarine is melted. Makes about 3 tbsp. (50 mL) sauce. Turn squash cut side up. Spoon about 1 tsp. (5 mL) sauce into each hollow. Spread in hollow. Bake for 10 minutes until edges are golden and sauce is syrupy. To serve, cut into quarters. Serves 8.

1 serving: 168 Calories; 6.3 g Total Fat; 229 mg Sodium; 2 g Protein; 30 g Carbohydrate; 4 g Dietary Fiber

Pictured on page 108.

Cashew Beans

Green beans delicately flavored with nuts and parsley.
Serve with Sirloin Casserole, page 91.

Frozen whole green beans (1/2 of 2 1/4 lbs., 1 kg, bag)	18 oz.	500 g
Boiling water	2 cups	500 mL
Salt	1/2 tsp.	2 mL
Sliced small fresh mushrooms	1/2 cup	125 mL
Chopped onion	1/4 cup	60 mL
Hard margarine (or butter)	2 tbsp.	30 mL
Salt	1/2 tsp.	2 mL
Coarsely chopped cashews	1/4 cup	60 mL
Chopped fresh parsley (or 3/4 tsp., 4 mL, flakes)	1 tbsp.	15 mL

Combine beans, boiling water and salt in large saucepan. Bring to a boil on medium-high. Reduce heat. Cover. Simmer for about 8 minutes until beans are tender-crisp. Drain. Set aside.

Sauté mushrooms and onion in margarine in frying pan on medium-high for about 4 minutes until onion is golden.

Add beans to mushroom mixture. Sprinkle salt over top. Stir until heated through. Turn into serving dish.

Sprinkle cashews and parsley over top. Makes 4 cups (1 L).

1/2 cup (125 mL): 77 Calories; 5.2 g Total Fat; 185 mg Sodium; 2 g Protein; 7 g Carbohydrate; 2 g Dietary Fiber

Pictured on front cover.

Side Dishes

Mustard Seed Pasta Side Dish

A simple side dish with mustard seeds flecked attractively throughout.
The feta cheese gives the dish an added sharpness and zip.
Serve with Oven-Fried Chicken, page 98.

Rotini (or fusilli) pasta (see Coach, below)	3 1/2 cups	875 mL
Boiling water	12 cups	3 L
Salt	1 tbsp.	15 mL
Black (or brown) mustard seeds	2 tsp.	10 mL
Hard margarine (or butter)	3 tbsp.	50 mL
Paprika	1/2 tsp.	2 mL
Ground turmeric	1/4 tsp.	1 mL
Crumbled feta cheese	1/3 cup	75 mL

Cook pasta in boiling water and salt in large uncovered pot or Dutch oven for 7 to 9 minutes until tender but firm. Drain. Return to pot. Cover to keep warm.

Heat mustard seeds in frying pan on medium for about 1 minute, stirring and watching carefully, until starting to pop. Remove from heat. Cover.

Once mustard seeds have stopped popping, add margarine, paprika and turmeric. Stir. Return to heat. Reduce heat to low. Heat and stir for about 1 minute until margarine is melted and bubbly. Pour over pasta.

Add cheese. Toss well. Serve immediately. Makes 4 1/2 cups (1.1 L).

1/2 cup (125 mL): 183 Calories; 5.9 g Total Fat; 115 mg Sodium; 6 g Protein; 26 g Carbohydrate; 1 g Dietary Fiber

Pictured on page 125.

To correctly substitute any pasta, *choose a pasta with similar size and/or cooking time to the one in the recipe. Check on the packaging to see if any significant size difference affects cooking time. If using a different size, be sure to use the same weight.*

Herbed Baby Potatoes

Who doesn't just love those little baby potatoes!
The herb and onion flavoring make this dish extra tasty.
Serve with Slow Cooker Beef Roast, page 92, or Lemon Cheese Fish, page 104.

Red (or white) baby potatoes (about 40), unpeeled	2 lbs.	900 g
Small onions, cut lengthwise into wedges	2	2
Hard margarine (or butter)	1 tbsp.	15 mL
Olive (or cooking) oil	1 tbsp.	15 mL
Lemon juice	1 tbsp.	15 mL
Italian (or Mediterranean) no-salt seasoning (such as Mrs. Dash)	1 tbsp.	15 mL
Seasoned salt	1/2 tsp.	2 mL

Fresh thyme leaves, for garnish

Cut larger potatoes in half to make all uniform in size. Place in greased 9 × 13 inch (22 × 33 cm) baking dish. Add onion.

Melt margarine in small saucepan on medium-low. Add next 4 ingredients. Stir. Pour over potato mixture. Toss until potato mixture is evenly coated with herbs. Cover tightly with foil. Bake in 375°F (190°C) oven for 40 minutes. Remove foil. Stir. Bake, uncovered, for 10 minutes until potatoes are tender and golden.

Sprinkle thyme leaves over top. Toss. Serves 8.

1 serving: 126 Calories; 3.3 g Total Fat; 99 mg Sodium; 3 g Protein; 22 g Carbohydrate; 2 g Dietary Fiber

Pictured on front cover.

HERBED POTATO SALAD: Prepare according to directions above. Chill. Cut potatoes and onion smaller if desired. Transfer to large bowl. Add 1/3 cup (75 mL) each sliced green onion and diced red pepper and 1/4 cup (60 mL) coarsely grated carrot. Toss. Combine 1/3 cup (75 mL) Italian dressing (your favorite) and 1 tbsp. (15 mL) lemon juice (or balsamic vinegar) in small bowl. Drizzle over potato mixture. Toss until well coated. Serve chilled or at room temperature. Will keep in refrigerator for up to 5 days.

Twisted Mashed Potatoes

Your guests will love the colorful swirls of carrot in these
incredible mashed potatoes. Serve with Oven-Fried Chicken, page 98.

Potatoes (about 4 medium), peeled and cut into large chunks	1 1/2 lbs.	680 g
Water	2 cups	500 mL
Salt	1/2 tsp.	2 mL
Hard margarine (or butter)	1 tbsp.	15 mL
Milk	1/4 cup	60 mL
Ground nutmeg	1/8 – 1/4 tsp.	0.5 – 1 mL
Large egg, fork-beaten	1	1
Medium carrots, cut into 1/2 inch (12 mm) slices	6	6
Water	1/2 cup	125 mL
Salt	1/4 tsp.	1 mL
Hard margarine (or butter)	1 tbsp.	15 mL
Large egg, fork-beaten	1	1

Paprika, sprinkle

Put potato, first amounts of water and salt into large saucepan. Bring to a boil on medium-high. Reduce heat to medium-low. Cover. Simmer for about 15 minutes until tender. Drain. Cool, with lid off, for 10 minutes.

Add first amount of margarine, milk, nutmeg and first egg to potato. Mash until smooth. Set aside.

Put carrot and second amounts of water and salt into separate large saucepan. Bring to a boil on medium-high. Reduce heat to medium-low. Cover. Simmer for 20 minutes, adding a bit more water if needed, until very tender. Do not drain. Cool, with lid off, for 10 minutes.

Add second amount of margarine and second egg to carrot with cooking water. Mash until smooth. Spoon carrot into 1 side of large resealable freezer bag. Spoon potatoes into other side of bag. Gently push together to meet in 1 corner. Eliminate large air spaces. Twist top of bag to enclose. Cut corner off bag, about 1 inch (2.5 cm) up. Gently squeeze bag, allowing potatoes and carrots to come out in a spiral pattern into greased shallow 1 quart (1 L) casserole.

(continued on next page)

Side Dishes

Sprinkle paprika over top. Bake, uncovered, in 350°F (175°C) oven for 40 minutes until edges are browned. Serves 6.

1 serving: 176 Calories; 5.9 g Total Fat; 203 mg Sodium; 5 g Protein; 27 g Carbohydrate; 3 g Dietary Fiber

Pictured on page 107.

Brown Rice Pilaf

*Nutty flavored brown rice with a light curry seasoning.
A nice side dish to serve with Easy Crumbed Fish, page 105,
or Pork Cutlets, page 109.*

Hard margarine (or butter)	2 tbsp.	30 mL
Long grain brown rice, uncooked	1 1/3 cups	325 mL
Chopped onion	1/2 cup	125 mL
Diced celery	1/3 cup	75 mL
Diced red pepper	1/3 cup	75 mL
Curry paste	1 tsp.	5 mL
Can of condensed chicken broth	10 oz.	284 mL
Water	1 3/4 cups	425 mL
Parsley flakes	1 tbsp.	15 mL
Chopped fresh parsley (or cilantro), or 3/4 tsp., 4 mL, flakes	1 tbsp.	15 mL

Melt margarine in large saucepan on medium-high. Add rice. Cook for about 5 minutes, stirring frequently, until rice starts to pop. Reduce heat to medium.

Add onion, celery, red pepper and curry paste. Sauté for 2 to 3 minutes until onion is slightly soft.

Add broth, water and parsley flakes. Stir. Bring to a boil on medium-high. Reduce heat to low. Cover. Cook for about 40 minutes until water is absorbed and rice is tender. Turn into serving bowl.

Sprinkle chopped parsley over rice mixture. Makes 5 cups (1.25 L).

1/2 cup (125 mL): 135 Calories; 3.7 g Total Fat; 223 mg Sodium; 4 g Protein; 22 g Carbohydrate; 1 g Dietary Fiber

Quick Vegetable Fried Rice

A side dish with Asian flair. Mixed vegetables add an appealing splash of color.
Enjoy this dish with Jiffy Chicken, page 98.

Cooking oil	1 tbsp.	15 mL
Large eggs, fork-beaten	2	2
Salt	1/4 tsp.	1 mL
Pepper	1/8 tsp.	0.5 mL
Frozen mixed vegetables, chopped if large	1 cup	250 mL
Green onions, sliced	2	2
Cooked long grain white rice, chilled (about 1 cup, 250 mL, uncooked)	3 cups	750 mL
Soy sauce	2 – 3 tbsp.	30 – 50 mL

Heat cooking oil in non-stick wok or frying pan on medium-high. Add eggs. Sprinkle salt and pepper over eggs. Cook for 30 to 40 seconds until starting to become firm. Quickly turn over with pancake flipper. Cook for a few seconds. Chop egg into small pieces using pancake flipper, or cook egg completely then transfer to cutting surface and chop. Reduce heat to medium.

Add vegetables and green onion to egg. Cook for 3 to 4 minutes, stirring occasionally, until vegetables are tender-crisp.

Add rice, breaking up any lumps with wet hands. Drizzle soy sauce over rice. Stir well. Cook for about 30 seconds, stirring frequently, until rice is hot and soy sauce has colored rice evenly. Makes 4 cups (1 L).

1/2 cup (125 mL): 157 Calories; 3.3 g Total Fat; 360 mg Sodium; 5 g Protein; 27 g Carbohydrate; 1 g Dietary Fiber

To make croutons, *cut 2 white bread slices into cubes. Heat 1 tbsp. (15 mL) olive (or cooking) oil in frying pan on medium-high for 1 minute. Add bread cubes. Stir-fry for 10 minutes until crisp and browned. Makes about 2 cups (500 mL). Seasonings (such as garlic salt, onion salt, seasoned salt or Parmesan cheese) can be added during stir-frying if desired.*

Side Dishes

Beef Parmesan

Beef steaks smothered in tangy pizza sauce and melted mozzarella cheese.
Serve with Baked Tomatoes, page 78.

Large egg	1	1
Water	2 tbsp.	30 mL
Seasoned croutons (see Coach, page 86)	2/3 cup	150 mL
Grated Parmesan cheese (see Coach, page 128)	1/4 cup	60 mL
Tenderized beef steaks (about 1 1/2 lbs., 680 g)	4	4
Cooking oil	1 tbsp.	15 mL
Can of pizza sauce	7 1/2 oz.	213 mL
Grated Parmesan cheese	1/3 cup	75 mL
Mozzarella cheese, sliced 1/4 inch (6 mm) thick (or 1/3 cup, 75 mL, grated)	8 oz.	225 g
Pepper, sprinkle (optional)		

Beat egg and water together in small bowl using fork.

Process croutons in blender until fine crumbs form.

Combine crumbs with first amount of Parmesan cheese in shallow dish.

Dip each steak into egg mixture. Press in crumb mixture to coat completely. Cook in cooking oil in frying pan on medium-high for about 5 minutes per side until browned.

Spread 1/2 of pizza sauce in 9 x 13 inch (22 x 33 cm) baking dish large enough to hold steaks in single layer. Arrange steaks on pizza sauce. Spoon remaining pizza sauce over top.

Sprinkle second amount of Parmesan cheese over sauce. Lay mozzarella cheese slices on each steak. Bake, uncovered, in 350°F (175°C) oven for about 30 minutes until heated through and cheese is melted.

Sprinkle pepper over individual servings. Serves 4.

1 serving: 667 Calories; 42.2 g Total Fat; 994 mg Sodium; 54 g Protein; 16 g Carbohydrate; 1 g Dietary Fiber

Pictured on front cover.

Burger Bash

Add your favorite burger toppings and serve with
Blue Cheese Caesar Salad, page 63, or Corn On The Cob, page 129.

Fine dry bread crumbs	1 cup	250 mL
Ketchup	1/2 cup	125 mL
Milk	1/4 cup	60 mL
Grated Parmesan cheese (see Coach, page 128)	1/4 cup	60 mL
Seasoned salt	1 tsp.	5 mL
Dried whole oregano	1 tsp.	5 mL
Dried sweet basil	1/2 tsp.	2 mL
Onion powder	1/2 tsp.	2 mL
Salt	1/2 tsp.	2 mL
Pepper	1/4 tsp.	1 mL
Lean ground beef	2 lbs.	900 g
Hamburger buns, split (buttered, optional)	8	8

Combine first 10 ingredients in large bowl.

Add ground beef. Mix well. Use 1/2 cup (125 mL) to shape each 3 inch (7.5 cm) patty. Cook in frying pan on medium for 5 to 6 minutes per side until no longer pink in center.

Serve patties in buns. Makes 8 burgers.

1 burger: 459 Calories; 21.1 g Total Fat; 989 mg Sodium; 28 g Protein; 37 g Carbohydrate; 1 g Dietary Fiber

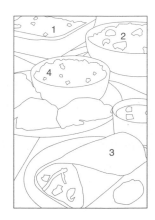

Lunch Choices

1. Cheese Strata, page 46
2. Pearly Shell Salad, page 61
3. Bean Burritos, page 42
4. Tasty Lettuce Wraps, page 131

Props Courtesy Of: Pfaltzgraff Canada

Main Dishes

Sirloin Casserole

A hearty casserole with creamy gravy and chunks of celery and mushrooms.
Perfect for a chilly evening. Serve with Cashew Beans, page 81.

Sirloin steak, cut into thin strips	1 lb.	454 g
Long grain white rice, uncooked	1/2 cup	125 mL
Can of condensed cream of mushroom soup	10 oz.	284 mL
Water	1 1/4 cups	300 mL
Sliced fresh mushrooms (or 10 oz., 284 mL, can, drained)	1 1/2 cups	375 mL
Sliced celery	1/3 cup	75 mL
Envelope of dry onion mushroom soup mix	1 1/4 oz.	38 g

Put steak strips into ungreased 2 quart (2 L) casserole. Sprinkle rice over beef.

Mix remaining 5 ingredients in medium bowl. Pour over rice. Cover. Bake in 350°F (175°C) oven for about 1 1/2 hours until steak strips and rice are tender. Serves 4.

1 serving: 387 Calories; 16.6 g Total Fat; 1534 mg Sodium; 26 g Protein; 32 g Carbohydrate; 1 g Dietary Fiber

Study Group Lunch

1. No-Bake Fudgy Brownies, page 59
2. Sour Cream And Cheese Biscuits, page 32
3. Cream Corn Chowder, page 75
4. Baby Pizzas, page 47
5. Pecan Chip Cookies, page 56

Main Dishes

Slow Cooker Beef Roast

Tender, moist roast slowly cooked with lots of rich, brown gravy.
Wonderful with Herbed Baby Potatoes, page 83.

Boneless sirloin tip roast	3 – 4 lbs.	1.4 – 1.8 kg
Envelope of brown gravy mix	3/4 oz.	25 g
Envelope of dry onion soup mix	1 1/4 oz.	38 g
Lemon lime soft drink	2 cups	500 mL
BEEFY ONION GRAVY		
Water		
Water	2/3 cup	150 mL
All-purpose flour	1/2 cup	125 mL

Set roast in 3 1/2 quart (3.5 L) slow cooker.

Combine gravy mix, soup mix and soft drink in small bowl. Pour over roast. Cover. Cook on low for 8 to 10 hours or on high for 4 to 5 hours until tender. Remove roast to serving plate.

Beefy Onion Gravy: Pour drippings, including fat, into 4 cup (1 L) liquid measure. Let stand for about 10 minutes until fat separates and comes to surface. Carefully spoon off and discard fat. Add water to drippings to make 4 cups (1 L). Pour into large saucepan or roasting pan. Bring to a boil on medium. Stir second amount of water into flour in small bowl until smooth. Stir into drippings for 5 to 7 minutes, stirring with whisk to prevent lumps, until boiling and thickened. Makes about 4 cups (1 L) gravy. Serve with roast. Makes twelve 3 oz. (85 g) servings.

1 serving: 215 Calories; 6.3 g Total Fat; 465 mg Sodium; 26 g Protein; 12 g Carbohydrate; trace Dietary Fiber

OVEN BEEF ROAST: Omit slow cooker. Place roast in small roasting pan. Cover. Bake in 225°F (110°C) oven for 3 1/2 to 4 hours until desired doneness. Makes twelve 3 oz. (85 g) servings.

Slow Cooker Tips:
✔ *Do not fill more than 3/4 full to allow food to expand and juices to form. This also prevents spillovers.*
✔ *Do not lift the lid once heat has built up. This will require 15 minutes more cooking time.*

Stuffed Peppers

Rice, meat and veggies all in one! Tender-crisp peppers
stuffed with flavorful Italian beef and rice.

Lean ground beef	1/2 lb.	225 g
Finely chopped onion	1 cup	250 mL
Finely chopped celery	1/2 cup	125 mL
Grated carrot	1/2 cup	125 mL
Instant rice, uncooked	1/2 cup	125 mL
Large egg	1	1
Italian seasoning	1 1/2 tsp.	7 mL
Salt	1/2 tsp.	2 mL
Pepper	1/8 tsp.	0.5 mL
Can of condensed tomato with basil and oregano soup	10 oz.	284 mL
Large green peppers, tops cut off, seeds and ribs removed (see Note)	4	4
Water	1/2 cup	125 mL

Scramble-fry first 4 ingredients together in frying pan on medium for 5 minutes until ground beef is no longer pink and vegetables are tender. Drain. Transfer to large bowl.

Add next 5 ingredients.

Add 1/2 of soup. Stir well. Makes 3 cups (750 mL) filling.

Stuff peppers with beef mixture. Arrange in ungreased 2 quart (2 L) casserole.

Combine remaining soup and water in small bowl. Pour over filling. Cover. Bake in 350°F (175°C) oven for 40 minutes. Remove cover. Bake for 30 minutes. Serves 4.

1 serving: 275 Calories; 7.7 g Total Fat; 889 mg Sodium; 16 g Protein; 37 g Carbohydrate; 5 g Dietary Fiber

Note: For more tender peppers, cover with water in large saucepan. Boil for 5 minutes. Drain. When cool enough to handle, proceed to stuff.

Zesty Beef Casserole

A zesty, colorful and fun dish for those who enjoy Mexican flavors.
Serve with Spinach Salad, page 62.

Lean ground beef	1 lb.	454 g
Chopped onion	1 cup	250 mL
Chopped green pepper	1/2 cup	125 mL
Chopped red pepper	1/2 cup	125 mL
Can of stewed tomatoes, with juice, chopped	14 oz.	398 mL
Medium egg noodles, uncooked	2 cups	500 mL
Can of kernel corn	12 oz.	341 mL
Can of diced green chilies, with liquid	4 oz.	113 g
Envelope of taco seasoning mix	1 1/4 oz.	35 g
Water	1 1/4 cups	300 mL
Salt	1/2 tsp.	2 mL
Pepper	1/4 tsp.	1 mL
Grated Monterey Jack With Jalapeño cheese	1 cup	250 mL

Sliced ripe olives, for garnish

Scramble-fry ground beef, onion and both peppers in frying pan on medium-high for about 5 minutes until beef is no longer pink. Drain.

Add tomatoes with juice. Stir. Turn into ungreased 3 quart (3 L) casserole.

Add next 7 ingredients. Stir. Cover. Bake in 350°F (175°C) oven for 30 minutes. Stir. Cover. Bake for 30 minutes until noodles are tender but firm.

Sprinkle with cheese. Bake, uncovered, for 5 minutes until cheese is melted.

Garnish with olives. Serves 6.

1 serving: 341 Calories; 14.1 g Total Fat; 1216 mg Sodium; 23 g Protein; 33 g Carbohydrate; 3 g Dietary Fiber

Pictured on page 36.

One-Dish Meal

Another all-in-one meal! A colorful beef, vegetable and pasta casserole with a rich, tasty gravy. Serve with a helping of crisp Cabbage Slaw, page 65.

Penne pasta	8 oz.	225 g
Boiling water	12 cups	3 L
Salt	1 tbsp.	15 mL
Lean ground beef	1 lb.	454 g
All-purpose flour	2 tbsp.	30 mL
Cans of condensed onion soup (10 oz., 284 mL, each)	2	2
Water	10 oz.	284 mL
Frozen peas and carrots	2 cups	500 mL
Can of sliced mushrooms, drained (or 2 cups, 500 mL, sliced fresh)	10 oz.	284 mL
French-fried onions	1/2 cup	125 mL

Cook pasta in boiling water and salt in large uncovered pot or Dutch oven for 7 to 10 minutes, stirring occasionally, until tender but firm. Drain. Turn into ungreased 2 quart (2 L) casserole.

Scramble-fry ground beef in frying pan on medium for about 5 minutes until no longer pink. Drain.

Sprinkle flour over beef. Mix well. Stir in soup and water until boiling and slightly thickened.

Add peas and carrots and mushrooms. Stir. Bring to a boil. Reduce heat to medium-low. Simmer, uncovered, for 2 minutes. Spoon over pasta. Bake in 350°F (175°C) oven for 30 to 35 minutes until heated through.

Scatter onions over top. Serves 6.

1 serving: 387 Calories; 11.4 g Total Fat; 1098 mg Sodium; 24 g Protein; 48 g Carbohydrate; 4 g Dietary Fiber

---

To prevent pasta from sticking *to bottom of pan, add to rapidly boiling water and immediately stir. Continue to stir occasionally during cooking time.*

Biscuit-Topped Casserole

Fluffy golden biscuit topping a beef casserole in a rich, creamy gravy.
This is delicious with Blue Cheese Caesar Salad, page 63.

Lean ground beef	1 lb.	454 g
Medium onion, chopped	1	1
Medium carrots, thinly sliced (about 1 1/4 cups, 300 mL)	2	2
Block of cream cheese, softened	4 oz.	125 g
Can of condensed cream of mushroom soup	10 oz.	284 mL
Milk	1/3 cup	75 mL
Salsa (or chili sauce)	1/4 cup	60 mL
Salt	1/2 tsp.	2 mL
Pepper	1/4 tsp.	1 mL
Refrigerator country-style biscuits (10 biscuits per tube)	12 oz.	340 g

Scramble-fry ground beef, onion and carrot in frying pan on medium-high for about 10 minutes until beef is no longer pink. Drain.

Stir cream cheese and 1/2 of soup in medium bowl until blended. Add remaining soup, milk, salsa, salt and pepper. Add beef mixture. Stir. Turn into ungreased 3 quart (3 L) casserole. Bake, uncovered, in 375°F (190°C) oven for 15 minutes.

Arrange biscuits over top. Bake for about 20 minutes until biscuits are golden. Serves 4.

1 serving: 620 Calories; 30.5 g Total Fat; 2188 mg Sodium; 32 g Protein; 55 g Carbohydrate; 2 g Dietary Fiber

Paré Pointer
She thinks a cartoon is what you sing in a car.

Main Dishes

Chicken à la King

Juicy chicken breasts with mushrooms and green peppers in a creamy sauce. This is delicious over noodles or on a bun, English muffin or toast. Tastes even better with a serving of Glazed Carrots, page 80, on the side.

Boneless, skinless chicken breast halves (about 4)	1 lb.	454 g
Water	2 cups	500 mL
Medium green pepper, finely chopped	1	1
Thinly sliced fresh mushrooms (or two 10 oz., 284 mL, cans, drained)	3 cups	750 mL
Hard margarine (or butter)	1 tbsp.	15 mL
CREAM SAUCE		
Hard margarine (or butter)	6 tbsp.	100 mL
All-purpose flour	1/3 cup	75 mL
Salt	1 tsp.	5 mL
Pepper	1/4 tsp.	1 mL
Milk	2 cups	500 mL

Cook chicken in water in medium saucepan on medium-high for about 15 minutes until no longer pink inside. Cool. Cut into bite-size pieces.

Sauté green pepper and mushrooms in margarine in frying pan on medium-high for about 7 minutes until soft.

Cream Sauce: Melt margarine in large saucepan on medium. Mix in flour, salt and pepper until smooth. Stir in milk. Heat and stir for about 3 minutes until boiling and thickened. Add chicken and green pepper mixture. Stir to heat through. Makes 4 1/2 cups (1.1 L). Serves 4.

1 serving: 426 Calories; 24 g Total Fat; 899 mg Sodium; 33 g Protein; 20 g Carbohydrate; 2 g Dietary Fiber

FANCIED-UP CHICKEN à la KING: Add 2 oz. (57 mL) jar chopped pimiento, drained, and 2 tbsp. (30 mL) sherry (or alcohol-free sherry), see Coach, page 48, to sauce with chicken. Serve 1/2 cup (125 mL) over 2 puff pastry patty shells per serving.

Pictured on page 108.

Oven-Fried Chicken

*An all-time favorite comfort food. Chicken drumsticks with
a crispy seasoned crumb coating. Serve with Mustard Seed Pasta Side Dish,
page 82, or Twisted Mashed Potatoes, page 84.*

Hard margarine (or butter)	1/4 cup	60 mL
Parsley flakes	1 tsp.	5 mL
Ground thyme	1/2 tsp.	2 mL
Dried tarragon leaves	1/4 tsp.	1 mL
Salt	1/2 tsp.	2 mL
Pepper	1/4 tsp.	1 mL
Coarsely crushed corn flakes cereal	1/2 cup	125 mL
Grated Parmesan cheese (see Coach, page 128)	1/4 cup	60 mL
Chicken drumsticks, skin removed	12	12

Microwave margarine in shallow microwave-safe bowl on high (100%) for about 30 seconds until melted. Add parsley, thyme, tarragon, salt and pepper. Stir.

Combine cereal and Parmesan cheese in separate shallow bowl.

Dip each drumstick into margarine mixture. Press into cereal mixture to coat completely. Arrange on greased foil-lined baking sheet. Bake in 400°F (205°C) oven for 40 to 45 minutes until juices run clear. Serves 4.

1 serving: 392 Calories; 24.1 g Total Fat; 596 mg Sodium; 38 g Protein; 4 g Carbohydrate; trace Dietary Fiber

Jiffy Chicken

Unique sauce is what makes this main dish great. Garnish with chopped green onion for added color. Serve with Quick Vegetable Fried Rice, page 86.

Boiling water	2 cups	500 mL
Orange pekoe tea bag	1	1
Soy sauce	3 tbsp.	50 mL
Liquid honey	1 tbsp.	15 mL
Boneless, skinless chicken breast halves (about 1 1/2 lbs., 680 g)	6	6

(continued on next page)

Pour boiling water over tea bag in frying pan. Press tea bag with spoon until water is tea colored. Remove tea bag.

Add soy sauce and honey. Stir well. Bring to a boil on medium. Add chicken. Cover. Cook for 15 minutes, turning chicken often, adding more tea if necessary. Remove cover. Keep sauce boiling. Cook for about 10 minutes, turning chicken occasionally, until sauce is reduced to 1/3 cup (75 mL). Serves 6.

1 serving: 143 Calories; 1.9 g Total Fat; 525 mg Sodium; 26 g Protein; 4 g Carbohydrate; 0 g Dietary Fiber

---

Divan-In-A-Pan

A mild curry-flavored dish with a generous offering of broccoli. The creamy sauce has a hint of mango.

Can of condensed cream of chicken and broccoli (or mushroom) soup	10 oz.	284 mL
Mayonnaise (not salad dressing), see Coach, page 61	1/2 cup	125 mL
Mango (or peach) chutney	1/4 cup	60 mL
Lemon juice	1 tsp.	5 mL
Chicken bouillon powder	1 tsp.	5 mL
Curry powder	1/2 tsp.	2 mL
Salt, just a pinch		
Cooking oil	1 tbsp.	15 mL
Boneless chicken breast fillets (or boneless, skinless chicken breast halves), cut into short strips	1 lb.	454 g
Bag of frozen chopped broccoli	15 oz.	500 g

Stir first 7 ingredients together vigorously in medium bowl. Set aside.

Heat cooking oil in frying pan on medium-high until hot. Add chicken. Stir-fry for about 6 minutes until lightly browned.

Add broccoli. Stir-fry for 4 to 5 minutes until broccoli is tender-crisp and chicken is tender. Add soup mixture. Heat and stir until boiling. Reduce heat to medium. Boil for 1 minute. Makes 4 3/4 cups (1.2 L). Serves 4.

1 serving: 491 Calories; 33.7 g Total Fat; 925 mg Sodium; 31 g Protein; 17 g Carbohydrate; 3 g Dietary Fiber

Chicken Teriyaki

The exotic Asian flavors of chicken with ginger and soy sauce will
make this a crowd pleaser. Serve with Asian-Style Vegetables, page 79.

Boneless, skinless chicken breast halves (about 1 lb., 454 g)	4	4
Low-sodium soy sauce	1/4 cup	60 mL
Finely grated gingerroot (or 1/4 tsp., 1 mL, ground ginger)	1 tsp.	5 mL
Granulated sugar	2 tbsp.	30 mL
Sherry (or alcohol-free sherry), see Coach, page 48	2 tbsp.	30 mL

Pound chicken with meat mallet or rolling pin until flat.

Mix soy sauce, ginger, sugar and sherry in large bowl. Add chicken. Stir. Cover. Marinate at room temperature for 20 minutes. Remove chicken. Discard marinade. Arrange chicken on greased baking sheet or broiler pan. Broil 4 inches (10 cm) from heat for about 3 minutes per side until tender and no longer pink inside. Serves 4.

1 serving: 164 Calories; 1.9 g Total Fat; 515 mg Sodium; 26 g Protein; 8 g Carbohydrate; trace Dietary Fiber

Oven-Baked Chicken

Lightly seasoned chicken drumsticks with a subtle paprika flavor.

All-purpose flour	1/3 cup	75 mL
Paprika	1 tsp.	5 mL
Seasoned salt	3/4 tsp.	4 mL
Salt	3/4 tsp.	4 mL
Pepper	1/4 tsp.	1 mL
Chicken drumsticks, skin removed	12	12

Combine first 5 ingredients in large resealable freezer bag.

(continued on next page)

Dampen chicken with water. Add a few pieces to bag. Seal bag. Shake until chicken is well coated. Arrange chicken in single layer on greased baking sheet. Repeat with remaining chicken and spice mixture. Bake in 425°F (220°C) oven for 30 minutes. Turn chicken. Bake for about 15 minutes until juices run clear. Serves 4.

1 serving: 281 Calories; 10.1 g Total Fat; 668 mg Sodium; 36 g Protein; 9 g Carbohydrate; trace Dietary Fiber

Pictured on page 107.

Easy Stir-Fry

Precut vegetables and an off-the-shelf sauce make this colorful and healthy meal fast and easy to prepare! The crisp vegetables and tangy sauce are delicious over rice.

Cooking oil	1 tbsp.	15 mL
Boneless chicken breast fillets (or boneless, skinless chicken breast halves), cut into short strips	3/4 lb.	340 g
Garlic clove, crushed (or 1/4 tsp., 1 mL, powder)	1	1
Chili paste (optional)	1/2 – 1 tsp.	2 – 5 mL
Precut stir-fry vegetables (or your own mixture)	4 cups	1 L
Can of sliced water chestnuts, drained	8 oz.	227 mL
Thick teriyaki basting sauce	2/3 cup	150 mL
Sherry (or alcohol-free sherry), see Coach, page 48	1 tbsp.	15 mL
Soy sauce	1 tbsp.	15 mL

Heat wok or frying pan until hot. Add cooking oil. Add chicken, garlic and chili paste. Stir-fry on medium-high for 1 to 2 minutes until chicken is half cooked.

Add vegetables and water chestnuts. Stir. Cover. Cook for 2 to 3 minutes until hot.

Stir in teriyaki sauce, sherry and soy sauce. Cover. Cook for 2 to 3 minutes until vegetables are tender-crisp. Stir until vegetables are coated completely. Makes about 4 cups (1 L).

1 cup (250 mL): 217 Calories; 5.1 g Total Fat; 2251 mg Sodium; 25 g Protein; 18 g Carbohydrate; 2 g Dietary Fiber

Macaroni Tomato Casserole

The addition of tangy tomato gives this version of macaroni and cheese a zesty twist. Serve as a satisfying vegetarian main course or as a tasty side dish. Serve with Red And Green Salad, page 63.

Elbow macaroni	1 1/2 cups	375 mL
Medium onion, chopped	1	1
Boiling water	8 cups	2 L
Cooking oil (optional)	1 1/2 tsp.	7 mL
Salt	2 tsp.	10 mL
Can of condensed tomato soup	10 oz.	284 mL
Can of diced tomatoes, with juice	14 oz.	398 mL
Water	1/2 cup	125 mL
Grated medium Cheddar cheese	1 cup	250 mL
Salt	1/2 tsp.	2 mL
Pepper	1/4 tsp.	1 mL
Grated medium Cheddar cheese	1 cup	250 mL

Cook macaroni and onion in boiling water, cooking oil and salt in large uncovered pot or Dutch oven for 5 to 7 minutes, stirring occasionally, until macaroni is tender but firm. Drain. Return macaroni and onion to pot.

Add next 6 ingredients. Stir. Turn into ungreased 3 quart (3 L) casserole.

Sprinkle second amount of cheese over top. Bake, uncovered, in 350°F (175°C) oven for about 30 minutes until hot. Serves 4.

1 serving: 477 Calories; 21.9 g Total Fat; 1359 mg Sodium; 23 g Protein; 49 g Carbohydrate; 3 g Dietary Fiber

Paré Pointer

It can be really hard to open the piano. All the keys are inside.

White Sauce

This variation of basic white sauce is versatile and especially good with fish and vegetables. True basic white sauce contains no onion salt or cayenne pepper.

Hard margarine (or butter)	2 tbsp.	30 mL
All-purpose flour	2 tbsp.	30 mL
Onion salt (or salt)	1/2 tsp.	2 mL
Pepper	1/8 tsp.	0.5 mL
Cayenne pepper, just a pinch		
Milk	1 cup	250 mL

Melt margarine in small saucepan on medium-low. Stir in flour until smooth. Add onion salt, pepper and cayenne pepper. Stir. Increase heat to medium-high.

Stir in milk. Heat and stir for about 3 minutes until boiling and thickened. Makes 1 cup (250 mL).

2 tbsp. (30 mL): 45 Calories; 3.1 g Total Fat; 119 mg Sodium; 1 g Protein; 3 g Carbohydrate; trace Dietary Fiber

Variation: Add 1/8 tsp. (0.5 mL) garlic powder or onion powder.

THIN WHITE SAUCE: Reduce margarine and flour to 1 tbsp. (15 mL) each.

THICK WHITE SAUCE: Increase margarine and flour to 3 tbsp. (50 mL) each.

CHEESE SAUCE: Add 1 cup (250 mL) grated medium Cheddar cheese. Stir until melted.

MUSTARD WHITE SAUCE: Add 1 1/2 tsp. (7 mL) dry mustard and 1/4 tsp. (1 mL) granulated sugar.

HERB WHITE SAUCE: Add 1/2 tsp. (2 mL) dill weed, parsley flakes or chives.

Smooth Sauces and Gravies: *Stir sauces and gravies constantly while heating and thickening to prevent lumps or burning.*

Lemon Cheese Fish

An easy-to-prepare fish dish in a tangy cream cheese sauce.
This succulent entrée tastes like you spent all day in the kitchen!
Serve with Herbed Baby Potatoes, page 83.

Package of frozen cod (or Boston bluefish) fillets, partially thawed	14 oz.	400 g
Hard margarine (or butter), softened	2 tsp.	10 mL
Lemon juice	1 tbsp.	15 mL
Block of cream cheese, chilled, cut into 8 pieces	4 oz.	125 g
Salt	1/4 tsp.	1 mL
Lemon pepper	1/4 tsp.	1 mL

Chopped fresh parsley, sprinkle

Separate cod into 4 portions. Blot dry. Arrange in single layer in greased shallow 2 quart (2 L) casserole. Spread margarine over fish portions. Sprinkle lemon juice over top. Bake, uncovered, in 400°F (205°C) oven for 10 minutes. Remove from oven.

Divide cream cheese among fish portions. Sprinkle with salt and lemon pepper. Bake, uncovered, for 5 minutes until cream cheese is soft and fish flakes easily when tested with fork. Mash and spread cream cheese over fish using fork.

Sprinkle parsley over top. Serves 4.

1 serving: 260 Calories; 18 g Total Fat; 335 mg Sodium; 22 g Protein; 1 g Carbohydrate; trace Dietary Fiber

Paré Pointer

Centipedes can't play football; by the time they
get their shoes on it's time to go home.

Main Dishes

Easy Crumbed Fish

A firm fish dish with a crispy herb and cheese-flavored topping.
Brown Rice Pilaf, page 85, is the perfect companion.

Package of frozen Boston bluefish (or other firm white fish) fillets, partially thawed	14 oz.	400 g
Buttery crackers (such as Ritz)	15	15
Italian no-salt seasoning (such as Mrs. Dash)	1 tsp.	5 mL
Hard margarine (or butter), melted	2 tbsp.	30 mL

Cut bluefish into about 16 pieces. Blot dry. Arrange in single layer in greased shallow 2 quart (2 L) casserole.

Put crackers into resealable freezer bag. Crush until coarse crumbs using rolling pin. Add seasoning. Shake well. Sprinkle over fish.

Drizzle margarine over crumb mixture. Bake, uncovered, in 450°F (230°C) oven for 10 to 12 minutes until fish flakes easily when tested with fork. Serves 4.

1 serving: 234 Calories; 12.9 g Total Fat; 240 mg Sodium; 21 g Protein; 7 g Carbohydrate; trace Dietary Fiber

Paré Pointer

A teacher says to spit out your gum while a train says to choo choo.

Simple Oven Dinner

Tender pork chops nestled on a bed of creamy rice.
Serve with Sweet Baked Squash, page 80.

Long grain white rice, uncooked	1 1/4 cups	300 mL
Envelope of dry vegetable soup mix	1 1/4 oz.	38 g
Can of condensed cream of mushroom (or wild mushroom) soup	10 oz.	284 mL
Can of condensed cream of asparagus soup	10 oz.	284 mL
Water	2 cups	500 mL
Boneless pork loin chops, trimmed of fat (see Coach, page 110)	8	8
Cooking oil	1 tbsp.	15 mL

Mix rice and soup mix in greased 4 quart (4 L) casserole or small roasting pan.

Mix both soups and water in medium bowl until smooth. Pour over rice. Stir well. Bake, uncovered, in 375°F (190°C) oven for 45 minutes. Stir well.

Brown pork chops, in 2 batches, in cooking oil in frying pan on medium-high for 3 to 4 minutes per side. Place pork chops on rice. Push down into liquid. Cover. Bake for 45 to 60 minutes until most of liquid has been absorbed and pork is tender. Serves 8.

1 serving: 331 Calories; 11.1 g Total Fat; 876 mg Sodium; 23 g Protein; 33 g Carbohydrate; 1 g Dietary Fiber

Variation: Omit pork chops. Use 12 boneless, skinless chicken breast halves (about 3 lbs., 1.4 kg).

Friends Over For Dinner

1. Fruit Pizza, page 134
2. Asian-Style Vegetables, page 79
3. Oven-Baked Chicken, page 100
4. Twisted Mashed Potatoes, page 84

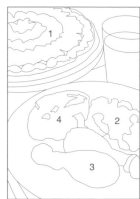

Main Dishes

Pork Cutlets

Tender pork cutlets in a rich sauce with a hint of wine and cheese.
Serve with Brown Rice Pilaf, page 85.

Boneless pork loin cutlets (about 1 1/2 lbs., 680 g)	6	6
Seasoned croutons (see Coach, page 86)	1 1/3 cups	325 mL
Pepper	1/4 tsp.	1 mL
Paprika	1/2 tsp.	2 mL
Large egg	1	1
Cooking oil	1 tbsp.	15 mL
Can of condensed broccoli and cheese soup	10 oz.	284 mL
Water	1/3 cup	75 mL
White (or alcohol-free) wine	1/3 cup	75 mL
Diced red pepper	1/2 cup	125 mL
Sliced green onion	1/3 cup	75 mL

Pound cutlets with meat mallet until very thin.

Put croutons, pepper and paprika into blender. Process until fine crumbs. Pour into shallow bowl.

Beat egg with fork in small bowl. Dip each cutlet into egg. Coat in crumb mixture. Brown in cooking oil in frying pan on medium-high for about 5 minutes per side.

Combine remaining 5 ingredients in medium bowl. Pour over and around cutlets. Cover. Simmer on medium-low for 20 to 25 minutes until juices from cutlets run clear. Serves 6.

1 serving: 326 Calories; 16.5 g Total Fat; 564 mg Sodium; 29 g Protein; 12 g Carbohydrate; 1 g Dietary Fiber

Pictured on page 125.

Romantic Dinner

1. Amaretto Strawberries, page 137
2. Sesame Soy Dressing, page 67
3. Sweet Baked Squash, page 80
4. Fancied-Up Chicken à la King, page 97

Props Courtesy Of: Dansk Gifts
Pfaltzgraff Canada

Pork Stir-Fry

This colorful dish is crisp, fresh and flavorful.
Serve with Asian-Style Vegetables, page 79.

SAUCE		
Water	1/4 cup	60 mL
Cornstarch	2 tbsp.	30 mL
Grape jelly preserves	1/3 cup	75 mL
Brown sugar, packed	2 tbsp.	30 mL
Soy sauce	2 tbsp.	30 mL
Garlic powder	1/4 tsp.	1 mL
Ground ginger	1/4 tsp.	1 mL
Cooking oil	1 tbsp.	15 mL
Boneless pork loin chops, trimmed of fat (see Coach, below) and cut into thin strips	3/4 lb.	340 g
Medium carrot, thinly sliced (about 1/2 cup, 125 mL)	1	1
Fresh pea pods (or 10 oz., 285 g, bag, frozen, thawed)	1 1/2 cups	375 mL
Slivered yellow or red pepper	2/3 cup	150 mL

Sauce: Stir water into cornstarch in small bowl until smooth. Add next 5 ingredients. Stir. Don't worry if slightly lumpy from the jelly, it will smooth out once heated. Set aside.

Heat wok or frying pan until hot. Add cooking oil. Add pork strips. Stir-fry on medium-high for 1 minute. Add carrot. Stir-fry for 1 to 2 minutes until desired doneness.

Add pea pods and yellow pepper. Stir-fry for 2 minutes until vegetables are tender-crisp. Stir sauce. Add to pork mixture. Heat and stir for about 1 minute until boiling and thickened. Makes 4 cups (1 L).

1 cup (250 mL): 316 Calories; 9.2 g Total Fat; 585 mg Sodium; 22 g Protein; 38 g Carbohydrate; 2 g Dietary Fiber

Trim the Fat! *To trim fat off pork chops, take a sharp knife and cut fat off around outside edge as close to meat as possible. If using for stir-fry, remove all the fat, but with other cooking methods, leave some on, depending on personal preference.*

Planned Leftovers

Build your confidence as a cook by planning ahead for several meals. Cook enough of a main meat so that you will have leftovers. Then have ingredients on hand to make two or three recipes using those leftovers. In this section, we have provided ideas using roast beef, chicken, salmon, pork, ham and even a stuffing!

Roast Beef

Beef covered with a tasty herb and spice rub. This size roast will serve six and allow leftovers for Shepherd's Pie, page 112, Roast Beef Chili, page 113, or Beef And Rice Milanese, page 114.

Inside round roast	3 – 4 lbs.	1.4 – 1.8 kg
HERB AND SPICE RUB		
Cooking oil	3 tbsp.	50 mL
Garlic cloves, minced (or 3/4 tsp., 4 mL, powder)	3	3
Pepper	1/2 tsp.	2 mL
Parsley flakes	2 tsp.	10 mL
Paprika	1 tsp.	5 mL
Seasoned salt	1 1/2 tsp.	7 mL
Cayenne pepper (optional)	1/4 tsp.	1 mL
Water	1/4 cup	60 mL

Pat roast dry with paper towel.

Herb And Spice Rub: Mix first 7 ingredients in small bowl until paste-like. Rub over top and sides of roast. Place roast, fat-side up, in medium roasting pan.

Pour water into roasting pan around roast. Cover. Roast in 300°F (150°C) oven for about 30 minutes per lb. (65 minutes per kg) for medium and about 48 minutes per lb. (110 minutes per kg) for well done until meat thermometer registers between 160°F (75°C) for medium and 170°F (77°C) for well done. Let stand for 10 minutes before carving. Makes six 3 oz. (85 g) servings, with 18 oz. (500 g) left over.

One 3 oz. (85 g) serving: 234 Calories; 14.1 g Total Fat; 213 mg Sodium; 25 g Protein; trace Carbohydrate; trace Dietary Fiber

Pictured on page 126.

Shepherd's Pie

This traditional comfort food is so simple using commercial instant potatoes.
Prepared in 15 minutes.

GRAVY

Chopped onion	1 cup	250 mL
Cooking oil	1 1/2 tsp.	7 mL
All-purpose flour	2 tbsp.	30 mL
Water	1 1/3 cups	325 mL
Beef bouillon powder	2 tsp.	10 mL
Worcestershire sauce	1 tsp.	5 mL
Salt, sprinkle		
Pepper, sprinkle		
Coarsely ground (or finely chopped) leftover Roast Beef, page 111	2 cups	500 mL
Frozen mixed vegetables, thawed	2 cups	500 mL

TOPPING

Boiling water	2 cups	500 mL
Hard margarine (or butter)	2 tbsp.	30 mL
Salt	1/4 tsp.	1 mL
Instant potato flakes	1 1/2 cups	375 mL
Grated sharp Cheddar cheese	1/2 cup	125 mL
Paprika, sprinkle		

Gravy: Sauté onion in cooking oil in frying pan on medium for 4 to 5 minutes until soft.

Sprinkle flour over onion mixture. Mix well. Stir in water for about 3 minutes until boiling and thickened.

Add bouillon powder, Worcestershire sauce, salt and pepper. Stir.

Add beef and vegetables. Stir well. Pack into greased 2 quart (2 L) casserole. Taste for salt and pepper, adding more if needed.

Topping: Stir boiling water, margarine and salt in small bowl until margarine melts.

Stir in potato flakes. Stir in cheese. Spread evenly over beef mixture. Make lines for decoration using fork tines.

(continued on next page)

112 Planned Leftovers

Sprinkle paprika over top. Bake, uncovered, in 350°F (175°C) oven for 35 to 40 minutes until hot and bubbly around edges. Serves 4 to 6.

1 serving: 413 Calories; 16.5 g Total Fat; 780 mg Sodium; 31 g Protein; 36 g Carbohydrate; 4 g Dietary Fiber

Pictured on page 126.

Roast Beef Chili

A hearty chili with a spicy bite to it. No one will guess it's leftovers.

Medium onion, chopped	1	1
Medium green pepper, chopped	1	1
Cooking oil	1 tbsp.	15 mL
Can of diced tomatoes, with juice	28 oz.	796 mL
Chili sauce	1/4 cup	60 mL
Worcestershire sauce	2 tsp.	10 mL
Chili powder	2 tsp.	10 mL
Salt	1/4 tsp.	1 mL
Pepper	1/4 tsp.	1 mL
Can of red kidney beans, with juice	14 oz.	398 mL
Coarsely ground (or finely chopped) leftover Roast Beef, page 111	2 cups	500 mL
Grated Cheddar cheese, for garnish		

Sauté onion and green pepper in cooking oil in large pot or Dutch oven on medium for about 5 minutes until onion is soft.

Add next 8 ingredients. Stir. Bring to a boil. Reduce heat. Simmer, uncovered, for 15 minutes, stirring occasionally, to blend flavors.

Sprinkle individual servings with cheese. Makes 7 cups (1.75 L).

1 cup (250 mL): 189 Calories; 4.9 g Total Fat; 679 mg Sodium; 17 g Protein; 20 g Carbohydrate; 6 g Dietary Fiber

Pictured on page 126.

Quick and easy gravy! *To avoid making gravy from scratch, use a 1 1/8 oz. (32 g) envelope of gravy mix. Prepare according to package directions.*

Beef And Rice Milanese

Parmesan cheese gives this dish a delightful lift.

Long grain white rice, uncooked	1 cup	250 mL
Finely chopped onion (about 1 small)	3/4 cup	175 mL
Hard margarine (butter browns too fast)	1/4 cup	60 mL
Water	2 1/2 cups	625 mL
Beef bouillon powder	1 tbsp.	15 mL
Coarsely chopped leftover Roast Beef, page 111	1 cup	250 mL
Pepper	1/4 tsp.	1 mL
Parsley flakes	1 tbsp.	15 mL
Grated Parmesan cheese (see Coach, page 128)	1/3 cup	75 mL

Fresh parsley, for garnish

Sauté rice and onion in margarine in frying pan on medium-high for about 5 minutes until both are golden.

Add next 5 ingredients. Cover. Bring to a boil. Reduce heat to medium-low. Simmer for about 15 minutes until liquid is absorbed and rice is tender.

Add Parmesan cheese. Stir until blended.

Garnish with parsley. Makes 4 cups (1 L).

1 cup (250 mL): 409 Calories; 17.4 g Total Fat; 781 mg Sodium; 19 g Protein; 43 g Carbohydrate; 1 g Dietary Fiber

Pictured on page 126.

Fresh herbs *are more flavorful and colorful than their dried counterparts, but dried herbs are more widely available year round. A general formula to convert fresh to dried is to use 4 parts fresh to 1 part dried. For example, use 1/4 tsp. (1 mL) dill weed in place of 1 tsp. (5 mL) fresh dill.*

Roast Chicken

Serve with Simple Stove-Top Stuffing, page 116, and cranberry sauce for an old-fashioned family dinner. The leftover chicken is delicious for Chicken Newburg, page 117, or Chicken Pot Pie, page 118. If you have any leftover gravy, use it for the gravy in Chicken Pot Pie, page 118.

Whole roasting chicken	5 lbs.	2.3 kg
Small onion, quartered	1	1
SIMPLE CHICKEN GRAVY		
Drippings		
Water, if necessary		
Water	1/2 cup	125 mL
All-purpose flour	3 tbsp.	50 mL
Chicken bouillon powder	1 tsp.	5 mL
Salt	1/4 tsp.	1 mL
Pepper	1/8 tsp.	0.5 mL

Wash chicken inside and out with cold running water. Pat dry with paper towels. Place onion in cavity of chicken. Tie wings with string to body. Tie legs to tail. Place, breast side up, in roasting pan. Cover with foil or roasting pan lid. Roast in 400°F (205°C) oven for 20 minutes. Reduce heat to 325°F (160°C). Roast for 1 1/2 to 2 hours until meat thermometer inserted in thigh, not touching bone, registers 190°F (88°C) and juices run clear when pierced with fork. Remove cover for last 15 minutes to brown. Remove chicken to serving plate.

Simple Chicken Gravy: Pour drippings, including fat, through sieve over 4 cup (1 L) liquid measure. Discard solids. Let drippings stand for 10 minutes until fat comes to surface. Carefully spoon off and discard fat. Add enough water to remaining drippings to make 1 1/3 cups (325 mL) in total. Pour into medium saucepan.

Stir second amount of water into flour, bouillon powder, salt and pepper in small bowl until smooth. Stir into drippings on medium for 5 to 7 minutes until boiling and slightly thickened. Makes about 1 2/3 cups (400 mL) gravy. Serve with chicken. Makes about 5 1/2 cups (1.4 L) cooked chicken, enough for four 1/2 cup (125 mL) servings with 3 1/2 cups (875 mL) left over.

One 1/2 cup (125 mL) serving with 1 tbsp. (15 mL) gravy: 202 Calories; 11.1 g Total Fat; 180 mg Sodium; 22 g Protein; 2 g Carbohydrate; trace Dietary Fiber

Simple Stove-Top Stuffing

A quick and easy homemade stuffing that is great with poultry, fish or vegetables. Serve with Roast Chicken, page 115, for a traditional dinner.

Chopped onion	1 cup	250 mL
Chopped celery, with leaves	1 cup	250 mL
Hard margarine (or butter)	1/3 cup	75 mL
Parsley flakes	1 tbsp.	15 mL
Poultry seasoning	1 1/2 tsp.	7 mL
Chicken bouillon powder	1 tsp.	5 mL
Salt	1/2 tsp.	2 mL
Pepper	1/4 tsp.	1 mL
Stale white bread slices, cubed (about 4 cups, 1 L)	7 – 8	7 – 8

Sauté onion and celery in margarine in frying pan on medium for about 5 minutes until onion is soft.

Mix next 5 ingredients in small bowl. Add to onion mixture. Heat and stir for about 1 minute until fragrant.

Add bread cubes. Stir for about 2 minutes until bread has absorbed liquid. Makes 4 cups (1 L).

1/2 cup (125 mL): 143 Calories; 9 g Total Fat; 456 mg Sodium; 2 g Protein; 14 g Carbohydrate; 1 g Dietary Fiber

SIMPLE BAKED STUFFING: Put stuffing into greased 2 quart (2 L) casserole. Cover. Bake in 325°F (160°C) oven for 30 minutes. Can buddy with chicken in the oven.

Paré Pointer

A dog can have fleas, but a flea can't have dogs.

Chicken Newburg

Lots of chicken and shrimp in creamy sauce with a hint of sherry.
A simple, yet elegant, dish for those with refined tastes.
Spoon over rice or noodles.

Finely chopped onion	1/2 cup	125 mL
Hard margarine (or butter)	3 tbsp.	50 mL
All-purpose flour	3 tbsp.	50 mL
Milk	1 3/4 cups	425 mL
Chicken bouillon powder	1 tsp.	5 mL
Salt	1/4 tsp.	1 mL
Pepper	1/8 tsp.	0.5 mL
Sherry (or alcohol-free sherry), see Coach, page 48	1/4 cup	60 mL
Coarsely chopped leftover Roast Chicken, page 115	2 cups	500 mL
Cooked medium shrimp (about 2/3 cup, 150 mL)	4 oz.	113 g

Sauté onion in margarine in frying pan on medium for about 5 minutes until soft.

Sprinkle flour over onion mixture. Mix well. Gradually stir in milk. Heat and stir for about 3 minutes until boiling and thickened.

Add bouillon powder, salt, pepper and sherry. Stir.

Add chicken and shrimp. Simmer, uncovered, for about 5 minutes, stirring frequently, until heated through. Makes 3 3/4 cups (925 mL).

2/3 cup (150 mL): 205 Calories; 9.7 g Total Fat; 362 mg Sodium; 20 g Protein; 7 g Carbohydrate; trace Dietary Fiber

Chicken Pot Pie

A hearty chicken stew hidden under golden biscuits.

Coarsely chopped leftover Roast Chicken, page 115	3 cups	750 mL
Coarsely chopped cooked potato	2 cups	500 mL
Frozen peas and carrots, thawed	1 1/2 cups	375 mL
Can of condensed cream of chicken soup	10 oz.	284 mL
Leftover Simple Chicken Gravy, page 115	1/2 cup	125 mL
Water	1/4 cup	60 mL
Dried thyme (or 1/4 tsp., 1 mL, poultry seasoning)	1/8 tsp.	0.5 mL
Dried sage	1/8 tsp.	0.5 mL
Salt	1/4 tsp.	1 mL
Pepper	1/8 tsp.	0.5 mL
TOPPING		
Biscuit mix	1 cup	250 mL
Milk	1/2 cup	125 mL
Large egg, fork-beaten	1	1

Toss first 3 ingredients together in ungreased 3 quart (3 L) casserole.

Mix next 7 ingredients in small bowl. Pour over chicken mixture. Stir well.

Topping: Measure biscuit mix into same small bowl. Stir in milk and egg until smooth. Carefully pour over chicken mixture. Bake, uncovered, in 400°F (205°C) oven for about 45 minutes until topping is golden and mixture is hot and bubbly. Serves 6.

1 serving: 374 Calories; 13.1 g Total Fat; 943 mg Sodium; 29 g Protein; 34 g Carbohydrate; 2 g Dietary Fiber

Stuffed Salmon

The leftovers from this dish are delicious in Salmon Loaf, page 119, or Salmon Cakes, page 120.

Whole salmon, pan ready (1 1/2 – 2 lbs., 680 – 900 g, each), see Coach, page 119	2	2
Box of long grain and wild rice stove-top stuffing mix, prepared according to package directions	4 1/4 oz.	120 g

(continued on next page)

Rinse salmon in cold water. Pat dry with paper towel. Lay each salmon on individual large sheets of greased foil. Divide and insert stuffing in fish. Measure thickest part. Fold foil around fish to seal completely. Place on ungreased baking sheet. Bake in 450°F (230°C) oven for 15 minutes per inch of thickness, plus additional 10 minutes for heat to penetrate foil. Fish is done when it flakes easily when tested with fork in thickest part. Makes six 3 oz. (85 g) servings, with 18 oz. (500 g) left over.

1 serving: 224 Calories; 10.6 g Total Fat; 805 mg Sodium; 24 g Protein; 8 g Carbohydrate; 1 g Dietary Fiber

Salmon Loaf

An attractive loaf with a refreshing tang of lemon. Uses leftover salmon and rice.

Large eggs	2	2
Lemon juice	1 tbsp.	15 mL
Fine dry bread crumbs	1 cup	250 mL
Flaked leftover Stuffed Salmon, page 118	1 1/2 cups	375 mL
(or two 7 1/2 oz., 213 g, cans red salmon,		
drained, skin and round bones removed)		
Milk	1/2 cup	125 mL
Salt	1 tsp.	5 mL
Pepper	1/4 tsp.	1 mL
Onion powder	1/4 tsp.	1 mL
Cooked long grain white rice (about	3/4 cup	175 mL
1/3 cup, 75 mL, uncooked)		

Beat eggs in medium bowl until frothy. Add remaining 8 ingredients. Stir well. Pack into greased 9 × 5 × 3 inch (22 × 12.5 × 7.5 cm) loaf pan. Bake, uncovered, in 350°F (175°C) oven for about 1 hour until golden and heated through. Serves 8.

1 serving: 144 Calories; 3.5 g Total Fat; 458 mg Sodium; 10 g Protein; 17 g Carbohydrate; 1 g Dietary Fiber

For pan-ready whole fish, *it should be cleaned (and gutted if necessary), scaled and head removed. To remove scales, hold fish under cold running water and run knife against grain of skin.*

Salmon Cakes

Delicate cakes with a crispy golden exterior.
These versatile treats are perfect for breakfast, lunch or dinner.

Large egg	1	1
Flaked leftover Stuffed Salmon, page 118	1 cup	250 mL
Mashed potato	1 cup	250 mL
Chopped green onion	2 tsp.	10 mL
Dill weed	1/2 tsp.	2 mL
Onion salt	1/4 tsp.	1 mL
Pepper	1/8 tsp.	0.5 mL
Hard margarine (or butter)	2 tbsp.	30 mL

Beat egg in small bowl using fork. Add next 6 ingredients. Mix well. Shape into 4 patties.

Melt margarine in frying pan on medium. Add patties. Brown for 4 to 5 minutes per side until golden. Makes 4 cakes.

1 cake: 178 Calories; 11.5 g Total Fat; 326 mg Sodium; 11 g Protein; 8 g Carbohydrate; trace Dietary Fiber

Variation: Omit green onion and dill weed. Add 1 tsp. (5 mL) each of finely grated lemon peel and parsley flakes.

Variation: Add 1/2 tsp. (2 mL) hot pepper.

Paré Pointer
Count Dracula's favorite food is fangfurters.

Planned Leftovers

Garlic-Stuffed Pork Roast

The garlic loses its pungent taste and turns sweet with roasting.
Use leftover pork in Pork Mix-Up, page 122, and Pork Hash, page 122.

Boneless pork loin roast	3 1/2 lbs.	1.6 kg
Garlic cloves, cut in half	8	8
Pepper	3/4 tsp.	4 mL
Dried whole oregano	1/4 tsp.	1 mL
Parsley flakes	1/4 tsp.	1 mL
Dried rosemary	1/4 tsp.	1 mL
Dried thyme	1/4 tsp.	1 mL
HERB GRAVY		
Drippings		
Water, if necessary		
Water	1 cup	250 mL
All-purpose flour	2 tbsp.	30 mL

Make 16 small slits at regular intervals in surface of roast with sharp knife. Insert garlic into slits. Put into small roasting pan.

Combine next 5 ingredients in small bowl. Rub over top and down sides of roast. Cover. Roast in 400°F (205°C) oven for 20 minutes. Reduce heat to 325°F (160°C). Roast 40 minutes per lb. (1 1/2 hours per kg) until meat thermometer registers 185°F (85°C) for well done. Remove and discard garlic if desired. Remove roast to serving plate.

Herb Gravy: Pour drippings, including fat, through sieve over 4 cup (1 L) liquid measure. Discard solids. Let drippings stand for 10 minutes until fat comes to surface. Carefully spoon off and discard fat. Add enough water to remaining drippings to make 1 cup (250 mL) in total. Pour into small saucepan.

Stir second amount of water into flour in small bowl until smooth. Stir into drippings. Heat and stir on medium for 5 to 7 minutes until boiling and thickened. Makes 2 cups (500 mL) gravy. Serve with roast. Makes six 3 oz. (85 g) servings, with 24 oz. (680 g) left over.

One 3 oz. (85 g) serving with about 2 tbsp. (30 mL) gravy: 121 Calories; 4.5 g Total Fat;
42 mg Sodium; 17 g Protein; 2 g Carbohydrate; trace Dietary Fiber

Pork Mix-Up

The addition of baked beans makes this a nutritious main course for lunch or supper. Serve this hearty dish as is or over rice or noodles.

Chopped onion	1 cup	250 mL
Cooking oil	1 tbsp.	15 mL
Cans of baked beans in tomato sauce (14 oz., 398 mL, each)	2	2
Diced leftover Garlic-Stuffed Pork Roast, page 121	2 cups	500 mL

Grated medium Cheddar cheese, for garnish

Sauté onion in cooking oil in frying pan on medium for about 7 minutes until onion is soft and begins to turn brown.

Add beans and pork. Reduce heat to medium-low. Heat and stir for about 10 minutes until heated through.

Sprinkle cheese over individual servings. Makes 4 cups (1 L).

1 cup (250 mL): 402 Calories; 11.7 g Total Fat; 893 mg Sodium; 32 g Protein; 47 g Carbohydrate; 17 g Dietary Fiber

Pork Hash

A dressed-up version of hash browns.
This is sweet, spicy and savory all at the same time.

Chopped onion	2/3 cup	150 mL
Diced red pepper	1/4 cup	60 mL
Hard margarine (or butter)	2 tbsp.	30 mL
Chopped cooked potato	2 cups	500 mL
Diced leftover Garlic-Stuffed Pork Roast, page 121	1 1/2 cups	375 mL
Can of kernel corn, drained (or 1 1/4 cups, 300 mL, frozen)	12 oz.	341 mL
Hot pepper sauce	1/2 tsp.	2 mL
Paprika	1/2 tsp.	2 mL
Salt	1/2 tsp.	2 mL

(continued on next page)

122   Planned Leftovers

Sauté onion and red pepper in margarine in frying pan on medium for about 7 minutes until onion is soft and begins to turn brown.

Add remaining 6 ingredients. Stir. Reduce heat to low. Cover. Cook for about 10 minutes, stirring once, until heated through. Makes 4 cups (1 L).

1 cup (250 mL): 315 Calories; 11.8 g Total Fat; 623 mg Sodium; 20 g Protein; 35 g Carbohydrate; 3 g Dietary Fiber

Baked Ham

The glaze and sauce take the ham from delicious to divine! With the leftover ham make Cheese Strata, page 46, Ham And Vegetable Frittata, page 124, Ham And Mushroom Soup, page 127, or Ham Dandy, page 128.

Boneless cooked ham	5 – 6 lbs.	2.3 – 2.7 kg
GLAZE		
Can of applesauce	14 oz.	398 mL
Apple cider vinegar	1 tbsp.	15 mL
Prepared mustard	2 tsp.	10 mL
Ground cloves	1/8 tsp.	0.5 mL

Put ham into small roasting pan. Cover. Bake in 325°F (160°C) oven for about 2 hours until meat thermometer registers 130°F (54°C). Drain.

Glaze: Combine all 4 ingredients in small bowl. Spoon about 1/2 cup (125 mL) over ham. Brush over sides to coat evenly. Increase heat to 350°F (175°C). Bake, uncovered, for 10 to 15 minutes until glaze has dried a bit. Put remaining glaze into small saucepan. Heat on medium until heated through. Serve with ham. Makes six 3 oz. (85 g) servings, with 42 oz. (1.2 kg) left over.

One 3 oz. (85 g) serving: 192 Calories; 9.4 g Total Fat; 1555 mg Sodium; 23 g Protein; 2 g Carbohydrate; trace Dietary Fiber

Paré Pointer

An autobiography is the life story of a car.

Ham And Vegetable Frittata

*A great brunch dish! The combination of ingredients is
as pretty as it is delicious. Serve with toast, salad or soup.*

Chopped onion	1/2 cup	125 mL
Chopped cooked potato	1/2 cup	125 mL
Chopped green pepper	1/2 cup	125 mL
Sliced fresh mushrooms	1/2 cup	125 mL
Salt	1/2 tsp.	2 mL
Pepper	1/8 tsp.	0.5 mL
Cooking oil	1/2 tbsp.	7 mL
Diced leftover Baked Ham, page 123	1/2 cup	125 mL
Large eggs, fork-beaten	6	6
Chopped tomato	1/2 cup	125 mL

Sauté first 6 ingredients in cooking oil in large frying pan on medium for
about 5 minutes until onion and green pepper are soft. Reduce heat to
medium-low.

Add ham. Heat and stir for 1 minute.

Pour eggs over ham mixture. Cover. Cook for about 10 minutes,
without stirring, until eggs are set. Loosen sides with spatula. Slide onto
serving dish.

Sprinkle tomato over top. Cuts into 6 wedges.

*1 wedge: 132 Calories; 7.4 g Total Fat; 448 mg Sodium; 10 g Protein; 6 g Carbohydrate;
1 g Dietary Fiber*

Pictured on page 71.

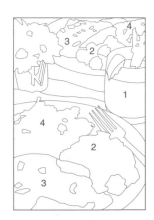

So, You're The Host
1. Classic Caesar, page 25
2. Glazed Carrots, page 80
3. Pork Cutlets, page 109
4. Mustard Seed Pasta Side Dish,
   page 82

Planned Leftovers

Ham And Mushroom Soup

A hearty soup of ham and mushrooms with a hint of thyme.
This is real rookie soup and doesn't require a lot of chopping.
For variety, add any leftover vegetables you have in the fridge.

Medium onion, chopped	1/2	1/2
Sliced fresh mushrooms	2 cups	500 mL
Cooking oil	1 1/2 tsp.	7 mL
Water	4 cups	1 L
Diced leftover Baked Ham, page 123	1 cup	250 mL
Frozen mixed vegetables (optional)	1/2 cup	125 mL
Vegetable bouillon powder	1 tbsp.	15 mL
Dried thyme	1/2 tsp.	2 mL
Parsley flakes	1/4 tsp.	1 mL
Garlic powder	1/8 tsp.	0.5 mL
Celery seed	1/8 tsp.	0.5 mL
Salt	1/4 tsp.	1 mL
Pepper	1/4 tsp.	1 mL

Sauté onion and mushrooms in cooking oil in large saucepan on medium for about 5 minutes until onion is soft.

Add remaining 10 ingredients. Bring to a boil on medium-high. Reduce heat. Cover. Simmer for 20 minutes, stirring occasionally. Makes 5 cups (1.25 L).

1 cup (250 mL): 95 Calories; 5.8 g Total Fat; 921 mg Sodium; 8 g Protein; 3 g Carbohydrate; 1 g Dietary Fiber

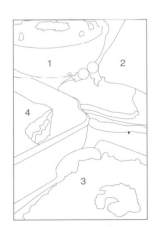

Planned Leftovers

1. Roast Beef Chili, page 113
2. Roast Beef, page 111
3. Beef And Rice Milanese, page 114
4. Shepherd's Pie, page 112

Ham Dandy

This creamy dish is very pretty when garnished
with green onion, parsley or diced tomato.

Broad egg noodles	3 cups	750 mL
Boiling water	8 cups	2 L
Salt	1/2 tsp.	2 mL
Hard margarine (or butter)	3 tbsp.	50 mL
All-purpose flour	3 tbsp.	50 mL
Chicken bouillon powder	1 tbsp.	15 mL
Pepper	1/4 tsp.	1 mL
Milk	1 3/4 cups	425 mL
Chopped leftover Baked Ham, page 123	1 cup	250 mL
Frozen peas	1/2 cup	125 mL
Grated Parmesan cheese (see Coach, below)	1/2 cup	125 mL

Cook noodles in boiling water and salt in large uncovered pot or Dutch oven on medium-high for 8 to 10 minutes, stirring occasionally, until tender but firm. Drain. Return to pot. Keep warm.

Melt margarine in medium saucepan on medium. Stir in flour, bouillon powder and pepper until smooth. Mix well. Gradually stir in milk. Heat and stir for about 3 minutes until boiling and thickened.

Add ham, peas and Parmesan cheese. Heat and stir until hot. Pour over noodles. Stir until noodles are coated. Makes 4 3/4 cups (1.2 L).

1 cup (250 mL): 345 Calories; 16 g Total Fat; 1242 mg Sodium; 20 g Protein; 30 g Carbohydrate; 2 g Dietary Fiber

Coach

Freshly grated Parmesan cheese *has better flavor, melts more evenly and looks nicer than the commercial pre-grated variety.*

Corn On The Cob

Sweet, fresh and buttery. A favorite summer treat for everyone and virtually no work to prepare. Serve with Burger Bash, page 88.

Medium corn cobs, in husk	3 – 4	3 – 4
Hard margarine (or butter), optional		
Salt, sprinkle (optional)		

Place cobs in microwave in triangle for 3 cobs or square for 4 cobs. Microwave, uncovered, on high (100%) for 3 minutes per cob. Remove husk.

Spread each cob with margarine. Sprinkle with salt. Makes 3 to 4 cobs.

1 cob: 131 Calories; 1.6 g Total Fat; 21 mg Sodium; 4 g Protein; 30 g Carbohydrate; 4 g Dietary Fiber

Micro-Chicken

Unbelievably fast—a main dish ready in 15 minutes! Serve with Baked Tomatoes, page 78.

Cooking oil	2 tbsp.	30 mL
Boneless, skinless chicken thighs	8	8
Seasoned salt	1/4 tsp.	1 mL
Medium onion, thinly sliced	1	1
Seasoned salt	1/4 tsp.	1 mL
Medium tomatoes, sliced	3	3
Grated medium Cheddar cheese	3/4 cup	175 mL

Measure cooking oil into microwave-safe casserole, large enough to hold chicken in single layer. Microwave, uncovered, on high (100%) for 30 seconds.

Set chicken in warmed cooking oil, turning once to grease tops. Sprinkle with first amount of seasoned salt. Scatter onion over chicken. Sprinkle with second amount of seasoned salt. Cover. Microwave on high (100%) for 7 minutes, turning casserole at halftime if microwave doesn't have turntable. Rearrange chicken at halftime so outside edges are now inside and inside edges are now outside.

Layer tomato over onion. Sprinkle cheese over tomato. Cover. Microwave on high (100%) for about 4 minutes until chicken is tender and no longer pink inside. Serves 4.

1 serving: 344 Calories; 21.4 g Total Fat; 297 mg Sodium; 30 g Protein; 7 g Carbohydrate; 2 g Dietary Fiber

Herb And Veggie Fusilli

Creamy pasta spirals with lots of vegetables. Prepare the sauce in the
microwave while the pasta cooks. Yummy with Tasty Cheese Loaf, page 31.

Fusilli pasta	1 1/2 cups	375 mL
Boiling water	8 cups	2 L
Salt	2 tsp.	10 mL
Olive (or cooking) oil	2 tsp.	10 mL
Hard margarine (or butter)	2 tsp.	10 mL
Garlic clove, crushed (or 1/4 tsp., 1 mL, powder)	1	1
Half-and-half cream	2/3 cup	150 mL
Frozen California vegetable mix	1 1/2 cups	375 mL
Frozen peas	3/4 cup	175 mL
Sliced fresh mushrooms	1/2 cup	125 mL
Finely grated Parmesan (or Romano) cheese (see Coach, page 128)	1/4 cup	60 mL
Chopped fresh parsley (or 1 1/2 tsp., 7 mL, flakes)	2 tbsp.	30 mL
Chopped fresh sweet basil (or marjoram), or 1 1/2 tsp. (7 mL), dried	2 tbsp.	30 mL
Pepper, sprinkle		

Cook pasta in boiling water and salt in large uncovered pot or Dutch oven for 8 to 10 minutes until tender but firm. Drain. Return to pot.

Drizzle with olive oil. Toss. Cover to keep warm.

Combine margarine, garlic and cream in 1 1/2 quart (1.5 L) microwave-safe dish. Microwave, uncovered, on high (100%) for about 2 minutes until margarine is melted and cream is almost boiling.

Add vegetable mix, peas and mushrooms. Stir. Cover. Microwave on high (100%) for 6 to 7 minutes until vegetables are tender-crisp. Pour over pasta.

Add Parmesan cheese, parsley, basil and pepper. Mix well. Cover. Let stand for 3 to 4 minutes until sauce is absorbed. Makes 4 1/2 cups (1.1 L).

1 cup (250 mL): 304 Calories; 10.2 g Total Fat; 201 mg Sodium; 12 g Protein; 42 g Carbohydrate; 4 g Dietary Fiber

LIGHT HERB AND VEGGIE FUSILLI: Omit half-and-half cream. Use same amount of skim (or 2%) evaporated milk.

Tasty Lettuce Wraps

Sweet and spicy teriyaki chicken and crunchy noodles wrapped
in cool, crisp lettuce leaves. Your friends will rave over these!

Lean ground chicken	1/2 lb.	225 g
Green onions, sliced	2	2
Diced celery	1/4 cup	60 mL
Diced red or green pepper	1/4 cup	60 mL
Coarsely grated carrot	1/4 cup	60 mL
Thick teriyaki sauce	1/3 cup	75 mL
Chili paste (or 1/8 tsp., 0.5 mL, cayenne pepper)	1 tsp.	5 mL
Instant noodle soup, noodles broken up, seasoning packet discarded	3 oz.	85 g
Iceberg lettuce leaves (see Note)	12	12

Combine first 5 ingredients in 1 1/2 quart (1.5 L) microwave-safe casserole. Cover. Microwave on high (100%) for 3 minutes, stirring at halftime to break up chicken.

Add teriyaki sauce and chili paste. Mix well. Microwave, uncovered, on high (100%) for 1 minute.

Add noodles. Toss. Makes about 2 1/2 cups (625 mL) filling.

To serve, spoon about 1 1/2 tbsp. (25 mL) into center of each lettuce leaf. Fold up, envelope-style. Serves 2 to 3.

1 serving: 447 Calories; 17.2 g Total Fat; 2040 mg Sodium; 30 g Protein; 43 g Carbohydrate; 2 g Dietary Fiber

Pictured on page 89.

Note: If leaves are quite large, tear in half, being sure the pieces are still large enough to roll.

To use a microwave safely and wisely...
- ✔ *Do not use metal or foil (not even twist ties) that hasn't been deemed safe.*
- ✔ *Use microwave-safe dishes.*
- ✔ *Use less time to prevent overcooking.*
- ✔ *Stir or rearrange partway through cooking because outside edges cook first.*
- ✔ *Allow food to stand a few minutes before serving as the food continues to cook after removal from microwave.*
- ✔ *Cover food (to prevent drying out and spattering).*

Crème de Menthe Cheesecake

A creamy mint-flavored cheesecake in a rich dark chocolate crumb pie shell.
Serve with a hot cup of coffee or a cool glass of milk.

CHOCOLATE PIE SHELL

Hard margarine (or butter)	1/4 cup	60 mL
Chocolate wafer crumbs	1 1/4 cups	300 mL
Granulated sugar (optional)	2 tbsp.	30 mL

FILLING

Cream cheese, softened	12 oz.	340 g
Granulated sugar	1/2 cup	125 mL
Large eggs	2	2
Mint-flavored liqueur (such as green Crème de Menthe)	1/3 cup	75 mL

TOPPING

Semisweet chocolate chips	1/2 cup	125 mL
Sour cream	1/2 cup	125 mL

Chocolate Pie Shell: Put margarine into 1 quart (1 L) microwave-safe bowl. Microwave, uncovered, on high (100%) for about 35 seconds until melted. Stir in wafer crumbs and sugar until well mixed. Press into bottom and up side of 9 inch (22 cm) glass pie plate. Microwave, uncovered, on high (100%) for 2 minutes. Set aside.

Filling: Beat cream cheese and sugar together in large bowl until smooth. Beat in eggs, 1 at a time, beating well after each addition. Add liqueur. Mix. Pour into pie shell. Cover with waxed paper. Microwave on medium (50%) for about 10 minutes, turning dish at halftime if microwave doesn't have turntable, until middle is set. Cool.

Topping: Put chocolate chips into 1 cup (250 mL) liquid measure. Microwave, uncovered, on medium (50%) for 2 minutes. Stir until smooth. Add sour cream. Stir. Spread over filling. Chill for 3 to 4 hours until set. Serves 8.

1 serving: 488 Calories; 31.8 g Total Fat; 341 mg Sodium; 7 g Protein; 41 g Carbohydrate; 1 g Dietary Fiber

Pictured on page 143.

Party Nut Nibblies

A variety of nuts tossed in a mildly spiced seasoning. Perfect for a party!

Hard margarine (or butter)	2 tbsp.	30 mL
Onion powder	1 tsp.	5 mL
Seasoned salt	1 tsp.	5 mL
Cayenne pepper	1/4 tsp.	1 mL
Garlic powder	1/4 tsp.	1 mL
Pecan halves	1 1/3 cups	325 mL
Almonds, with skin	1 1/3 cups	325 mL
Unsalted cashews	1 1/3 cups	325 mL

Combine first 5 ingredients in large microwave-safe bowl. Microwave, uncovered, on high (100%) for 30 seconds. Stir until combined and margarine is melted.

Add pecans, almonds and cashews. Toss until nuts are coated. Microwave, uncovered, on medium (50%) for about 15 minutes, stirring every 5 minutes, until nuts are toasted. Remove to paper towels to absorb excess margarine. Cool. Makes 4 cups (1 L).

1/4 cup (60 mL): 220 Calories; 20 g Total Fat; 95 mg Sodium; 5 g Protein; 8 g Carbohydrate; 2 g Dietary Fiber

Pictured on page 17.

OVEN NUT NIBBLIES: Spread nut mixture on baking sheet. Bake, uncovered, in 350°F (175°C) oven for 5 to 10 minutes, stirring occasionally, until toasted.

Coach

Microwave oven models *can vary quite a bit in their features. These variances will affect cooking times. Some basic differences are:*

✔ *interior size (small, medium or large)*
✔ *turntable (or not)*
✔ *power (watts)*
✔ *settings (number of settings; how settings are stated, whether by number or name; preset cook and defrost options)*

The recipes in The Rookie Cook *were tested in microwaves with 700 watts of power.*

Fruit Pizza

Wow everyone with this soft, chewy, cookie-like crust topped with creamy filling and delectable fresh fruit. Make this colorful and refreshing dessert a few hours ahead.

CRUST		
Yellow cake mix (1 layer size)	1	1
Large egg, fork-beaten	1	1
Water	2 tbsp.	30 mL
Hard margarine (or butter), softened	2 tbsp.	30 mL
Brown sugar, packed	2 tbsp.	30 mL
Finely chopped walnuts	1/4 cup	60 mL
FILLING		
Cream cheese, softened	12 oz.	340 g
Icing (confectioner's) sugar	3/4 cup	175 mL
Vanilla	1 tsp.	5 mL
TOPPING		
Seedless red grapes	20	20
Ripe honeydew melon, sliced	1/2	1/2
Can of mandarin orange segments (10 oz., 284 mL, size), drained	1/2	1/2
Fresh strawberries, sliced	4	4
Seedless purple grapes, halved	3	3
GLAZE		
Apricot jam (or orange marmalade)	1/4 cup	60 mL
Water	1 tbsp.	15 mL

Crust: Mix all 6 ingredients well in large bowl. Press in greased 12 inch (30 cm) pizza pan, forming rim around edge. Bake in 350°F (175°C) oven for about 15 minutes until wooden pick inserted in center comes out clean. Cool.

Filling: Beat cream cheese, icing sugar and vanilla together in medium bowl until smooth and fluffy. Spread over cooled crust.

Topping: Arrange fruit over cream cheese mixture to make an attractive pattern.

(continued on next page)

Glaze: Stir jam and water in small cup until combined. Microwave, uncovered, on high (100%) for 10 to 15 seconds until liquefied. Pour through sieve. Discard solids. Dab surface of fruit with glaze to give shine and to prevent fruit from drying out. Serves 10 to 12.

1 serving: 374 Calories; 19.5 g Total Fat; 288 mg Sodium; 6 g Protein; 47 g Carbohydrate; 2 g Dietary Fiber

Pictured on page 107.

Strawberry Cheese Tarts

These tantalizing summer treats make the perfect BBQ or picnic dessert.
These tarts are best served the day they are made. An easy recipe to double.
A great rookie recipe from Company's Coming Pies.

Semisweet chocolate chips	1/3 cup	75 mL
Hard margarine (or butter)	1 tbsp.	15 mL
Unbaked tart shells, baked according to package directions and cooled	12	12
Block of cream cheese, softened	4 oz.	125 g
Granulated sugar	1/2 cup	125 mL
Sour cream	3 tbsp.	50 mL
Orange flavoring	1/4 tsp.	1 mL
Vanilla	1/4 tsp.	1 mL
TOPPING		
Sliced fresh strawberries	1 cup	250 mL
Strawberry (or other red) jelly, melted	2 tbsp.	30 mL

Heat and stir chocolate chips and margarine together in small heavy saucepan on medium-low for about 3 minutes until melted. Divide and spoon into bottom of tart shells. Chill until set.

Beat cream cheese, sugar and sour cream together in small bowl for about 5 minutes until smooth.

Mix in orange flavoring and vanilla. Divide and spoon over chocolate. Chill for about 1 hour until set.

Topping: Toss strawberries and jelly in small bowl until strawberries are coated. Divide and spoon over cream cheese mixture. Chill. Makes 12 tarts.

1 tart: 178 Calories; 10.7 g Total Fat; 126 mg Sodium; 2 g Protein; 20 g Carbohydrate; 1 g Dietary Fiber

Pictured on front cover.

Chilled Chocolate Dessert

A chocolate pudding-like filling on a firm cookie-like crust.

CRUST		
All-purpose flour	2 cups	500 mL
Hard margarine (or butter), softened	1/2 cup	125 mL
Brown sugar, packed	1/2 cup	125 mL
Baking powder	1 tsp.	5 mL
Vanilla	1 tsp.	5 mL
Salt	1/4 tsp.	1 mL
Large egg, fork-beaten	1	1
FILLING		
Envelopes of dessert topping (not prepared)	2	2
Milk	2/3 cup	150 mL
Block of cream cheese, softened	8 oz.	250 g
Brown sugar, packed	1 cup	250 mL
Instant chocolate pudding powder (4 serving size)	1	1
Milk	1 1/2 cups	375 mL

Grated chocolate (optional)

Crust: Mix all 7 ingredients in medium bowl until crumbly. Press evenly in bottom of ungreased 9 x 13 inch (22 x 33 cm) pan. Bake in 350°F (175°C) oven for 12 to 15 minutes until edges are golden. Cool.

Filling: Beat dessert topping and first amount of milk together in medium bowl until stiff peaks form. Set aside.

Beat cream cheese and brown sugar together in separate medium bowl until smooth. Fold in 1/2 of dessert topping. Spread over cooled crust.

Beat pudding powder and second amount of milk together in small bowl until smooth. Spoon over cream cheese mixture. Chill for about 5 minutes until set.

Spread remaining dessert topping over pudding. Sprinkle chocolate over dessert topping. Chill for at least 3 to 4 hours. Cuts into 24 pieces.

1 piece: 218 Calories; 9.7 g Total Fat; 210 mg Sodium; 3 g Protein; 30 g Carbohydrate; trace Dietary Fiber

Pictured on page 35 and on back cover.

Amaretto Strawberries

For that "little something" after a heavy meal.
The Romans valued the strawberry for its reputed therapeutic powers.
To our modern eye, the visual benefits of the strawberries in this dish are clear!

Sliced small fresh strawberries	2 cups	500 mL
Almond-flavored liqueur (such as Amaretto)	1/4 cup	60 mL
Scoops of vanilla ice cream	4	4

Combine strawberries and liqueur in medium bowl. Cover. Marinate at room temperature for 3 to 4 hours, stirring occasionally.

Serve over ice cream in small individual bowls. Serves 4.

1 serving: 229 Calories; 8 g Total Fat; 57 mg Sodium; 3 g Protein; 29 g Carbohydrate; 2 g Dietary Fiber

Pictured on page 108.

Kulfi Ice Cream

Pronounced KOOHL-fee. A simple, rich dessert from India that is sweet, milky and crunchy. An ice-cream maker can be used if you have one.

Evaporated milk (see Coach, page 45)	1 1/2 cups	375 mL
Can of sweetened condensed milk	11 oz.	300 mL
Whipping cream	1 cup	250 mL
Almond flavoring	1/4 tsp.	1 mL
Pistachios, slivered (or chopped)	10	10
Almonds, slivered (or chopped)	10	10

Combine all 6 ingredients in medium bowl. Pour into foil-lined 9 x 9 inch (22 x 22 cm) pan. Mixture should be about 1 inch (2.5 cm) thick. Lining pan with foil makes it easier to lift ice cream out. Freeze until firm or freeze in ice-cream maker according to manufacturer's directions. Cut with hot sharp knife. Cuts into 18 squares.

2 squares: 312 Calories; 18.7 g Total Fat; 112 mg Sodium; 8 g Protein; 30 g Carbohydrate; trace Dietary Fiber

Pictured on page 143.

Easy Bake Cheesecake

The four distinct layers of this dessert are
impressive in both taste and appearance.

GRAHAM CRUMB CRUST

Hard margarine (or butter)	1/3 cup	75 mL
Graham cracker crumbs	1 1/4 cups	300 mL
Granulated sugar	2 tbsp.	30 mL

FILLING

Cream cheese, softened	12 oz.	340 g
Granulated sugar	3/4 cup	175 mL
Large eggs	3	3

TOPPING

Sour cream	1 cup	250 mL
Granulated sugar	1/4 cup	60 mL
Can of cherry pie filling	19 oz.	540 mL

Graham Crumb Crust: Melt margarine in medium saucepan on medium. Add graham crumbs and sugar. Stir until well mixed. Press evenly in bottom of ungreased 9 × 9 inch (22 × 22 cm) pan.

Filling: Beat cream cheese, sugar and eggs together in medium bowl until smooth. Pour over crust. Bake in 350°F (175°C) oven for 25 minutes until set. Cool for 10 minutes.

Topping: Stir sour cream and sugar together in small bowl. Spread evenly over cream cheese mixture. Bake for 8 minutes. Cool for 1 hour.

Spread with pie filling. Chill. Cuts into 12 pieces.

1 piece: 369 Calories; 20.3 g Total Fat; 231 mg Sodium; 5 g Protein; 43 g Carbohydrate;
1 g Dietary Fiber

Pictured on page 143.

Paré Pointer

Upon his arrival home, E.T.'s mother asked,
"Where on earth have you been?"

Cherry Chilled Cheesecake

*An attractive rosy-colored dessert that combines the
favorite flavors of cream cheese and cherries.*

GRAHAM CRUMB CRUST

Hard margarine (or butter)	1/3 cup	75 mL
Graham cracker crumbs	1 1/4 cups	300 mL
Brown sugar, packed	2 tbsp.	30 mL

FILLING

Block of cream cheese, softened	8 oz.	250 g
Icing (confectioner's) sugar	1 1/2 cups	375 mL
Vanilla	1/2 tsp.	2 mL
Can of cherry pie filling	19 oz.	540 mL

TOPPING

Frozen whipped topping, thawed (or whipped cream)	2 cups	500 mL

Graham Crumb Crust: Melt margarine in medium saucepan on medium.
Add graham crumbs and brown sugar. Stir until well mixed. Reserve
3 tbsp. (50 mL) crumb mixture. Press remaining crumb mixture evenly in
bottom of ungreased 9 x 9 inch (22 x 22 cm) pan. Bake in 350°F (175°C)
oven for 10 minutes. Cool.

Filling: Beat cream cheese, icing sugar and vanilla together in medium
bowl until smooth and fluffy.

Add pie filling. Stir. Turn into crust. Spread evenly.

Topping: Spread whipped topping evenly over pie filling mixture. Sprinkle
reserved crumb mixture over top. Chill for several hours or overnight. Cuts
into 12 pieces.

*1 piece: 329 Calories; 17 g Total Fat; 189 mg Sodium; 3 g Protein; 43 g Carbohydrate;
1 g Dietary Fiber*

Pictured on page 144.

To prevent cracks in cheesecakes, *run knife around top edge
between cheesecake and pan immediately after removing from oven.
This will allow cheesecake to settle evenly as it cools. Cracks are also
caused by overbeating when adding eggs.*

Turtle Pie

A lavish indulgence of caramel, chocolate and nuts.
This rich dessert won't last long!

FILLING

Chocolate pudding powder (not instant), 6 serving size	1	1
Milk	2 cups	500 mL
Thick caramel (or butterscotch) ice cream topping	1/3 cup	75 mL
Graham Crumb Crust, page 138	1	1
Pecan halves, chopped	2/3 cup	150 mL

TOPPING

Frozen whipped topping, thawed	1 1/2 cups	375 mL
Thick caramel (or butterscotch) ice cream topping	2 tbsp.	30 mL
Chopped pecans	2 tbsp.	30 mL

Filling: Combine pudding powder and milk in medium saucepan. Heat and stir on medium for about 10 minutes until boiling. Remove from heat. Let stand at room temperature for 20 minutes, stirring often.

Pour ice cream topping into crust. Gently spread to cover bottom. Sprinkle with pecans. Pour pudding over pecans. Cover with plastic wrap directly on surface to prevent film from forming. Chill for about 1 1/2 hours until set.

Topping: Remove plastic wrap. Spread whipped topping over filling. Drizzle with ice cream topping. Sprinkle pecans over top. Cuts into 8 wedges.

1 wedge: 429 Calories; 20.6 g Total Fat; 350 mg Sodium; 5 g Protein; 60 g Carbohydrate; 1 g Dietary Fiber

Pictured on page 144.

Perfect Pastry Tips:

✔ *Use cold or ice water and cold shortening or lard.*
✔ *Wrap and chill pastry before rolling out.*
✔ *Do not overmix or overwork pastry or it will be tough. Pastry will also be tough if there isn't enough fat in proportion to flour.*
✔ *Do not let pastry get too warm as you work it or it will shrink when baked.*
✔ *Make more rather than less as you can always freeze any leftover pastry dough.*

Desserts

Cookie Crumb Crust

A versatile golden crust that can be used as a base for many sweet fillings, such as Frozen Lemon Cream Pie, page 145.

Hard margarine (or butter)	1/3 cup	75 mL
Vanilla wafer crumbs	1 1/3 cups	325 mL
Granulated sugar	2 tbsp.	30 mL

Melt margarine in small saucepan on medium. Add wafer crumbs and sugar. Stir until well mixed. Press in bottom and up side of 9 inch (22 cm) pie plate. Bake in 350°F (175°C) oven for 8 to 10 minutes until golden. Makes 1 pie crust.

1/8 of crust: 146 Calories; 10.2 g Total Fat; 138 mg Sodium; 1 g Protein; 14 g Carbohydrate; 0 g Dietary Fiber

Pictured on page 143.

Cooking Oil Pastry

An easy no-fail pastry. Use as a dessert crust in Rustic Peach And Blueberry Pie, page 142, or as a savory appetizer pastry in Curried Beef Samosas, page 20.

All-purpose flour	4 cups	1 L
Baking powder	2 tbsp.	30 mL
Salt	1 tsp.	5 mL
Cooking oil	1 cup	250 mL
Cold water	1 cup	250 mL

Combine flour, baking powder and salt in large bowl.

Add cooking oil and cold water. Mix with fork until dough forms a ball. Divide into 4 balls. Use immediately or cover with plastic wrap and chill. Makes enough pastry for 2 double-crust pie shells (about 1 lb., 454 g, pastry).

1/16 of crust: 248 Calories; 14.7 g Total Fat; 288 mg Sodium; 3 g Protein; 26 g Carbohydrate; 1 g Dietary Fiber

Pictured on page 144.

Rustic Peach And Blueberry Pie

A perfect recipe for the rookie cook. It's very easy yet looks like a pastry chef baked it. The juicy sweet peaches are nice with the slightly tart blueberries.

Cooking Oil Pastry, page 141 (or other double-crust pie pastry)	1/2	1/2
Brown sugar, packed	1/3 cup	75 mL
All-purpose flour	2 tbsp.	30 mL
Ground cinnamon	1/4 tsp.	1 mL
Frozen sliced peaches, thawed, drained	4 cups	1 L
Fresh (or frozen, thawed) blueberries	2 cups	500 mL
Icing (confectioner's) sugar	1 tbsp.	15 mL

Shape pastry into large circle on lightly floured surface. Roll out to about 16 inches (40 cm) in diameter. Transfer to ungreased 12 inch (30 cm) pizza pan allowing excess pastry to hang over sides.

Combine brown sugar, flour and cinnamon in large bowl. Add peaches and blueberries. Stir until coated with flour mixture. Turn out onto center of pastry. Spread out and arrange in even layer to within 4 inches (10 cm) of pastry edges. Bring pastry up and over fruit to cover several inches around edge. Pleat or fold excess pastry around inner edge. Bake in 375°F (190°C) oven for about 45 minutes until crust is golden and fruit is tender. Cool to warm room temperature.

Dust exposed fruit and top edge of pastry with icing sugar. Serves 12.

1 serving: 313 Calories; 10 g Total Fat; 200 mg Sodium; 3 g Protein; 55 g Carbohydrate; 3 g Dietary Fiber

Pictured on page 144.

Dessert Buffet
1. Easy Bake Cheesecake, page 138
2. Crème de Menthe Cheesecake, page 132
3. Frozen Lemon Cream Pie, page 145, with Cookie Crumb Crust, page 141
4. Kulfi Ice Cream, page 137

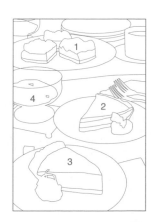

Frozen Lemon Cream Pie

A simple light dessert to follow a heavy main course.
The cold, crisp, lemon flavor is the perfect sweet ending.

Package of lemon-flavored gelatin (jelly powder)	3 oz.	85 g
Granulated sugar	2 tbsp.	30 mL
Boiling water	1 cup	250 mL
Freshly squeezed lemon juice (about 2 medium lemons)	1/3 – 1/2 cup	75 – 125 mL
Finely grated lemon peel	2 tsp.	10 mL
Vanilla ice cream, softened	2 cups	500 mL
Cookie Crumb Crust, page 141 (or commercial 9 inch, 22 cm, deep graham cracker crust)	1	1

Combine gelatin and sugar in medium bowl. Add boiling water. Stir until gelatin and sugar are dissolved.

Add lemon juice and lemon peel. Stir. Chill for about 1 1/2 hours, stirring and scraping down sides occasionally, until thick and syrupy. Do not let gelatin set too firmly or mixture will be lumpy when ice cream is added.

Add ice cream. Stir gently until smooth. Spoon into crust. Spread evenly. Cover with plastic wrap. Freeze for at least 8 hours or overnight. Cuts into 8 wedges.

1 wedge: 273 Calories; 14 g Total Fat; 193 mg Sodium; 3 g Protein; 36 g Carbohydrate; trace Dietary Fiber

Pictured on page 143.

To Make Ahead: Wrap in foil. Freeze. Can be frozen for up to 8 weeks.

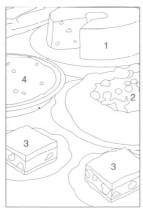

Choose Your Dessert

1. Strawberries And Cream Cake, page 148
2. Rustic Peach And Blueberry Pie, page 142, with Cooking Oil Pastry, page 141
3. Cherry Chilled Cheesecake, page 139
4. Turtle Pie, page 140

Props Courtesy Of: Anchor Hocking Canada
Casa Bugatti

Banana Cake

A lovely, moist homemade base that can be made into a delicious layer cake. Drizzle with Peanut Butter Sauce, page 149, if desired.

Hard margarine (or butter), softened	1/2 cup	125 mL
Granulated sugar	1 1/4 cups	300 mL
Large eggs	2	2
Vanilla	1 tsp.	5 mL
All-purpose flour	2 cups	500 mL
Baking powder	2 1/2 tsp.	12 mL
Baking soda	1/2 tsp.	2 mL
Salt	1/4 tsp.	1 mL
Mashed banana (about 3 medium), see Coach, below	1 1/2 cups	375 mL

Cream margarine, sugar, eggs and vanilla together in large bowl until light and fluffy.

Combine flour, baking powder, baking soda and salt in medium bowl.

Add flour mixture to margarine mixture in 3 additions, alternating with banana in 2 additions, beginning and ending with flour mixture. Beat on low until batter is smooth. Turn into 2 greased 8 inch (20 cm) round pans. Bake in 350°F (175°C) oven for 25 minutes until wooden pick inserted in center comes out clean. Cool in pans for 5 minutes before turning out onto wire racks to cool. Makes one 2 layer cake. Cuts into 16 wedges.

1 wedge: 208 Calories; 6.9 g Total Fat; 214 mg Sodium; 3 g Protein; 35 g Carbohydrate; 1 g Dietary Fiber

BANANA MUFFINS: Prepare Banana Cake batter, above. Fill muffin cups 3/4 full. Bake in 350°F (175°C) oven for 15 to 17 minutes until wooden pick inserted in center of muffin comes out clean. Cool in pan for 5 minutes before removing to wire racks to cool. Makes 2 dozen muffins.

Coach

Before bananas get too ripe, *mash, put into freezer bag or container in 1 cup (250 mL) amounts, and freeze. Banana may darken but that only makes for a better-colored and stronger-flavored final product.*

Chocolate Cake

*A one-bowl cake—just beat it! The rich chocolaty flavor is irresistible.
Ice with Cream Cheese Icing, page 148.*

All-purpose flour	1 1/2 cups	375 mL
Granulated sugar	1 1/4 cups	300 mL
Cocoa, sifted if lumpy (see Coach, below)	1/2 cup	125 mL
Baking powder	1 tsp.	5 mL
Baking soda	1 tsp.	5 mL
Salt	1/2 tsp.	2 mL
Hard margarine (or butter), softened	1/2 cup	125 mL
Large eggs	2	2
Vanilla	1 tsp.	5 mL
Hot water	1 cup	250 mL

Measure all 10 ingredients into large bowl in order given. Beat on low until
moistened. Beat on medium for about 1 minute, scraping down sides of
bowl, until smooth. Turn into greased 9 x 9 inch (22 x 22 cm) pan. Bake in
350°F (175°C) oven for about 35 minutes until wooden pick inserted in
center comes out clean. Cool in pan for 5 minutes before turning out onto
wire rack to cool. Cuts into 16 pieces.

*1 piece: 180 Calories; 7.2 g Total Fat; 257 mg Sodium; 3 g Protein; 28 g Carbohydrate;
1 g Dietary Fiber*

Lumps in cocoa *will not necessarily break up when stirred.
Sift the measured amount of cocoa before adding to recipe to
break up any lumps.*

Strawberries And Cream Cake

A dessert that is as beautiful as it is delicious! This cake freezes well—only a few minutes from freezer to plate. A special treat for unexpected guests.

Package of strawberry-flavored gelatin (jelly powder)	3 oz.	85 g
Boiling water	1 cup	250 mL
Frozen strawberries in syrup, partially thawed	15 oz.	425 g
Large angel food cake	1	1
Carton of vanilla ice cream, softened	2 qt.	2 L

Put gelatin into medium bowl. Add boiling water. Stir until gelatin is dissolved. Add strawberries and syrup. Stir. Chill for about 5 minutes until slightly thickened.

Tear or cut cake with bread knife into 1 inch (2.5 cm) cubes. Put into large bowl. Pour thickened gelatin mixture over cake cubes. Fold in ice cream. Transfer to two-piece 4 1/2 × 10 inch (11 × 25 cm) angel food tube pan. Freeze. Unmold before serving. Cuts into 20 slices.

1 slice: 189 Calories; 6.3 g Total Fat; 183 mg Sodium; 3 g Protein; 31 g Carbohydrate; 1 g Dietary Fiber

Pictured on page 144.

Variation: Omit frozen strawberries. Use 2 cups (500 mL) mashed fresh strawberries and 1 tbsp. (15 mL) granulated sugar.

Variation: Add 2 to 3 tbsp. (30 to 50 mL) almond or orange-flavored liqueur (such as Amaretto or Grand Marnier) to slightly thickened gelatin mixture.

Cream Cheese Icing

An icing classic—fluffy and sweet. The perfect icing to crown Chocolate Cake, page 147, or your favorite carrot cake recipe.

Block of cream cheese, softened	4 oz.	125 g
Icing (confectioner's) sugar	3 cups	750 mL
Hard margarine (or butter), softened	3 tbsp.	50 mL
Vanilla	1 tsp.	5 mL

(continued on next page)

Desserts

Beat all 4 ingredients together on low in medium bowl until moistened. Beat on medium until light and fluffy. Makes 1 3/4 cups (425 mL).

1 tbsp. (15 mL): 77 Calories; 2.7 g Total Fat; 27 mg Sodium; trace Protein; 13 g Carbohydrate; 0 g Dietary Fiber

Chocolate Sauce

A very quick, easy and decadent chocolate sauce. Perfect to dress up ice cream or crêpes or to drizzle over Peanut Butter Loaf, page 34. Serve hot or cold.

Granulated sugar	1 cup	250 mL
Cocoa, sifted if lumpy (see Coach, page 147)	6 tbsp.	100 mL
Skim evaporated milk (see Coach, page 45)	3/4 cup	175 mL
Salt	1/8 tsp.	0.5 mL

Stir sugar and cocoa together in small saucepan. Add evaporated milk and salt. Stir until smooth. Bring to a boil on medium. Remove from heat. Cool to room temperature. Makes 1 1/3 cups (325 mL).

2 tbsp. (30 mL): 95 Calories; 0.5 g Total Fat; 50 mg Sodium; 2 g Protein; 23 g Carbohydrate; 1 g Dietary Fiber

Peanut Butter Sauce

A nutty pick-me-up for ice cream. Will stiffen when chilled so bring to room temperature before serving. Enjoy drizzled over a piece of Banana Cake, page 146.

Water	1/3 cup	75 mL
Smooth peanut butter	1/3 cup	75 mL
Corn syrup	1/4 cup	60 mL

Measure all 3 ingredients into small bowl. Stir until smooth. Store in airtight container. Makes about 1 cup (250 mL).

2 tbsp. (30 mL): 87 Calories; 5.1 g Total Fat; 59 mg Sodium; 3 g Protein; 9 g Carbohydrate; 1 g Dietary Fiber

CRUNCHY CHOCOLATE PEANUT SAUCE: Omit smooth peanut butter. Use crunchy peanut butter. Add 2 tbsp. (30 mL) chocolate syrup. Makes 1 1/4 cups (300 mL).

Measurement Tables

Throughout this book measurements are given in Conventional and Metric measure. To compensate for differences between the two measurements due to rounding, a full metric measure is not always used. The cup used is the standard 8 fluid ounce. Temperature is given in degrees Fahrenheit and Celsius. Baking pan measurements are in inches and centimetres as well as quarts and litres. An exact metric conversion is given below as well as the working equivalent (Metric Standard Measure).

Spoons

Conventional Measure	Metric Exact Conversion Millilitre (mL)	Metric Standard Measure Millilitre (mL)
1/8 teaspoon (tsp.)	0.6 mL	0.5 mL
1/4 teaspoon (tsp.)	1.2 mL	1 mL
1/2 teaspoon (tsp.)	2.4 mL	2 mL
1 teaspoon (tsp.)	4.7 mL	5 mL
2 teaspoons (tsp.)	9.4 mL	10 mL
1 tablespoon (tbsp.)	14.2 mL	15 mL

Cups

Conventional Measure	Metric Exact Conversion Millilitre (mL)	Metric Standard Measure Millilitre (mL)
1/4 cup (4 tbsp.)	56.8 mL	60 mL
1/3 cup (5 1/3 tbsp.)	75.6 mL	75 mL
1/2 cup (8 tbsp.)	113.7 mL	125 mL
2/3 cup (10 2/3 tbsp.)	151.2 mL	150 mL
3/4 cup (12 tbsp.)	170.5 mL	175 mL
1 cup (16 tbsp.)	227.3 mL	250 mL
4 1/2 cups	1022.9 mL	1000 mL (1 L)

Oven Temperatures

Fahrenheit (°F)	Celsius (°C)
175°	80°
200°	95°
225°	110°
250°	120°
275°	140°
300°	150°
325°	160°
350°	175°
375°	190°
400°	205°
425°	220°
450°	230°
475°	240°
500°	260°

Dry Measurements

Conventional Measure Ounces (oz.)	Metric Exact Conversion Grams (g)	Metric Standard Measure Grams (g)
1 oz.	28.3 g	28 g
2 oz.	56.7 g	57 g
3 oz.	85.0 g	85 g
4 oz.	113.4 g	125 g
5 oz.	141.7 g	140 g
6 oz.	170.1 g	170 g
7 oz.	198.4 g	200 g
8 oz.	226.8 g	250 g
16 oz.	453.6 g	500 g
32 oz.	907.2 g	1000 g (1 kg)

Pans

Conventional Inches	Metric Centimetres
8x8 inch	20x20 cm
9x9 inch	22x22 cm
9x13 inch	22x33 cm
10x15 inch	25x38 cm
11x17 inch	28x43 cm
8x2 inch round	20x5 cm
9x2 inch round	22x5 cm
10x4 1/2 inch tube	25x11 cm
8x4x3 inch loaf	20x10x7.5 cm
9x5x3 inch loaf	22x12.5x7.5 cm

Casseroles

CANADA & BRITAIN Standard Size Casserole	Exact Metric Measure	UNITED STATES Standard Size Casserole	Exact Metric Measure
1 qt. (5 cups)	1.13 L	1 qt. (4 cups)	900 mL
1 1/2 qts. (7 1/2 cups)	1.69 L	1 1/2 qts. (6 cups)	1.35 L
2 qts. (10 cups)	2.25 L	2 qts. (8 cups)	1.8 L
2 1/2 qts. (12 1/2 cups)	2.81 L	2 1/2 qts. (10 cups)	2.25 L
3 qts. (15 cups)	3.38 L	3 qts. (12 cups)	2.7 L
4 qts. (20 cups)	4.5 L	4 qts. (16 cups)	3.6 L
5 qts. (25 cups)	5.63 L	5 qts. (20 cups)	4.5 L

Photo Index

Coach Index

Recipe Index

153

154

Company's Coming cookbooks are available at retail locations throughout Canada!

EXCLUSIVE mail order offer on next page
Buy any 2 cookbooks—choose a 3rd FREE of equal or less value than the lowest price paid.

Original Series — CA$15.99 Canada — US$12.99 USA & International

CODE		CODE		CODE	
SQ	150 Delicious Squares	SC	Slow Cooker Recipes	RC	The Rookie Cook
CA	Casseroles	ODM	One-Dish Meals	RHR	Rush-Hour Recipes
MU	Muffins & More	ST	Starters	SW	Sweet Cravings
SA	Salads	SF	Stir-Fry	YRG	Year-Round Grilling
AP	Appetizers	MAM	Make-Ahead Meals	GG	Garden Greens
SS	Soups & Sandwiches	PB	The Potato Book	CHC	Chinese Cooking
CO	Cookies	CCLFC	Low-Fat Cooking	PK	The Pork Book
PA	Pasta	CCLFP	Low-Fat Pasta	RL	Recipes For Leftovers
BA	Barbecues	CFK	Cook For Kids	EB	The Egg Book
PR	Preserves	SCH	Stews, Chilies & Chowders	SDP	School Days Parties
CH	Chicken, Etc.	FD	Fondues	HS	Herbs & Spices
KC	Kids Cooking	CCBE	The Beef Book	BEV	The Beverage Book **NEW**
CT	Cooking For Two	CB	The Cheese Book		*October 1/04*

Lifestyle Series

CODE	CA$17.99 Canada US$15.99 USA & International
DC	Diabetic Cooking

CODE	CA$19.99 Canada US$15.99 USA & International
HC	Heart-Friendly Cooking
DDI	Diabetic Dinners

Special Occasion Series

CODE	CA$20.99 Canada US$19.99 USA & International
GFK	Gifts from the Kitchen

CODE	CA$22.99 Canada US$19.99 USA & International
WC	Weekend Cooking

CODE	CA$24.99 Canada US$19.99 USA & International
BSS	Baking—Simple to Sensational **NEW**
	September 1/04

Most Loved Recipe Collection

CODE	CA$23.99 Canada US$19.99 USA & International
MLA	Most Loved Appetizers
MLMC	Most Loved Main Courses

Company's Coming
COOKBOOKS®

Company's Coming Publishing Limited
2311 – 96 Street
Edmonton, Alberta, Canada T6N 1G3
Tel: 780-450-6223 Fax: 780-450-1857
www.companyscoming.com

EXCLUSIVE Mail Order Offer
See previous page for list of cookbooks

Buy 2 Get 1 FREE!
Buy any 2 cookbooks—choose a **3rd FREE**
of equal or less value than the lowest price paid.

Quantity	Code	Title	Price Each	Price Total
			$	$
		DON'T FORGET to indicate your FREE BOOK(S). (see exclusive mail order offer above) please print		
TOTAL BOOKS (including FREE)		**TOTAL BOOKS PURCHASED:**	$	

	International	Canada & USA
Plus Shipping & Handling (per destination)	$11.98 (one book)	$5.98 (one book)
Additional Books (including FREE books)	$ ($4.99 each)	$ ($1.99 each)
Sub-Total	$	$
Canadian residents add G.S.T.(7%)		$
TOTAL AMOUNT ENCLOSED	$	$

The Fine Print

- Orders outside Canada must be **PAID IN US FUNDS** by cheque or money order drawn on Canadian or US bank or by credit card.
- Make cheque or money order payable to: **Company's Coming Publishing Limited**.
- Prices are expressed in Canadian dollars for Canada, US dollars for USA & International and are subject to change without prior notice.
- Orders are shipped surface mail. For courier rates, visit our web-site: **www.companyscoming.com** or contact us: **Tel: 780-450-6223 Fax: 780-450-1857**.
- Sorry, no C.O.D.'s.

Gift Giving

- Let us help you with your gift giving!
- We will send cookbooks directly to the recipients of your choice if you give us their names and addresses.
- Please specify the titles you wish to send to each person.
- If you would like to include your personal note or card, we will be pleased to enclose it with your gift order.
- Company's Coming Cookbooks make excellent gifts: Birthdays, bridal showers, Mother's Day, Father's Day, graduation or any occasion …collect them all!

☐ MasterCard   ☐ VISA

Expiry date

Account #

Name of cardholder

Cardholder's signature

Shipping Address
Send the cookbooks listed above to:

Name:

Street:

City: Prov./State:

Country: Postal Code/Zip:

Tel: (   )

Email address:

☐ YES! Please send a catalogue